Ecotourism in North East India

Ecotourism in North East India

(With Reference to Arunachal Pradesh)

Maila Lama

Anshah Publishing House

Rs. 600; US$ 30

ISBN: 978-81-8364-104-3

First Published in India in 2014

Ecotourism in North East India:
With Reference to Arunachal Pradesh

Published by:
ANSHAH PUBLISHING HOUSE
LG, Pankaj Central Market, I.P. Ext.,
Patparganj, Delhi-110092, Tel: 22235152, 9810522367
Br.Off. 4617/18, Ansari Road, Darya Ganj,
New Delhi-110002, Tel: 9650028065

Foreword

Ecotourism is a way to travel to natural areas that takes responsibility to conserve the environment and sustain well-being of local communities. Ecotourism came into prominence in the late eighties as a strategy for reconciling conservation with development in ecologically rich areas. Dr. Maila Lama has responded to the call of the time by undertaking present valuable study. I am happy to present and introduce this book entitled *Ecotourism in North East India: With Reference to Arunachal Pradesh.* The present volume is a forward looking work on the inter-linkages of environment and ecotourism in general and Arunachal Pradesh, in particular, which have enormous wealth of forests and wildlife resources and rich biodiversity and need careful attention for appropriate strategy for the utilization of these resources without much environmental degradation.

The book discusses the socio-economic characteristics of tourists in Arunachal Pradesh, as well as analyses the structure of tourists demand in the region. However, it concentrates on estimating the recreational value of tourism and identifies the possible negative impacts of tourism on environment as well as the enormous potential gains of tourism. The development of environmental friendly infrastructure, mainstreaming local crafts and culture into ecotourism and most importantly benefits sharing to local communities are important. If these are taken care of with other lessons learnt from the region and other parts of the country, Arunachal Pradesh can usher in a socially acceptable, environmentally sustainable and economically beneficial ecotourism in the State.

The book will be a valuable source of information for the environmental economists, environmentalists, the students of tourism and finally the policy makers. My congratulations to Dr. Maila Lama for this useful volume.

(Prof. Amitava Mitra)
Rajiv Gandhi University
Arunachal Pradesh

Acknowledgements

This book would not have seen the light of the day without the support of many people and institutions that I came across during the course of my research study, especially, Prof. Amitava Mitra, who gave much needed valuable guidance and support. Much thanks and respect to him.

I am also thankful to officers and staffs of Tourism Department, Government of Arunachal Pradesh for their cooperation and help.

I owe greatly to my parents, Shri Shyam Lama and Smt. Thuli Lama for their whole hearted support and guidance. I am also indebted to my beloved wife Smt. Sange Chojom for her moral support and bearing with me during this study.

I am also thankful to Mr. D. Kumar of Anshah Publishing House for kind acceptance of manuscript and bringing out this book in given time.

Maila Lama

Contents

List of Tables and Figures

LIST OF TABLES

LIST OF FIGURES

One
Introduction

The term 'Ecotourism' emerged in the late 1980s as a direct result of the world's acknowledgement and reaction to sustainable practices and global ecological practices (Diamantis *et al.*, 1999). It is generally used to describe nature based travel to undisturbed areas having educative value. A variety of definition exists for the term ecotourism. However, the earliest and the most widely used definition of ecotourism was given by Ceballos–Lascurain in 1987 who defined it as, "tourism that involves traveling to relatively undisturbed or uncontaminated natural areas with the specific objective of studying, admiring and enjoying the scenery and its wild plants and animals as well as any existing cultural manifestations (both past and present) found in these areas" (Boo, 1990, p. 20).

The Ecotourism Society in 1991 defined ecotourism as, "purposeful travel to natural areas to understand the culture and natural history of the environment, taking care not to alter the integrity of ecosystem while producing economic opportunities that make the conservation of natural resources beneficial to local people". The society, later, shortened this definition of ecotourism to "responsible travel to natural areas which conserves the environment and improves the welfare of local people" (Western, 1993, p. 8).

Valentine (1993) defined ecotourism as that kind of tourism which is based on relatively undisturbed natural areas, non-damaging, non-degrading, ecologically sustainable, a direct contributor to the continued protection and management of the natural areas and subject to an adequate and appropriate management regime.

The National Ecotourism Strategy (Commonwealth Department of Tourism, 1994) defined ecotourism as "ecotourism is a nature-based tourism that involves education and interpretation of the natural environment and is managed to be ecologically sustainable". It notes that ecotourism should be ecologically sustainable, provide visitor satisfaction, local benefits and be appropriate to its environmental and cultural setting.

All these definitions suggest that ecotourism is dependent on natural environment for certain types of activities and is careful of the natural environment. The International Society's definition of ecotourism makes local benefits a requirement for tourism to be classified as ecotourism. Benefits of ecotourism to local people by generating income can create a local incentive to conserve natural areas. Ecotourism is often interchanged with nature tourism. However, nature tourism is primarily concerned with the direct enjoyment of some relatively undisturbed phenomenon of nature and lacks any explicit conservation motive (Valentine, 1993). Ecotourism is a nature-based tourism that must enhance or maintain natural systems. Ecotourism usually refers to non-consumptive use of natural based and wildlife related recreation activities such as bird watching, wildlife watching, nature photography, botanical study, and wildlife treks or safaris (Whelan, 1991).

Ecotourism can contribute to economic development of a destination especially in its role of earning foreign exchange, diversifying regional economies, and in providing income and employment directly to local people. Ecotourism, if properly managed, can provide additional revenues to public and private managers as well as offer additional justifications for managing the resource base for sustainable use. Proper development of ecotourism can also promote the preservation of cultural and social values, including historical places of interest that might otherwise be lost. This is true because ecotourism promotes culturally and ecologically sensitive travel.

TOURISM, ECONOMICS AND CONSERVATION

Tourism is one of the world's largest industries and ecotourism is the fastest growing segment of the tourism industry (Whelan, 1991). An estimate made by United Nations World

Tourism Organization (UNWTO) shows that the global spending on ecotourism increased by 20 per cent per year, about five times the average rate of growth in tourism industry as a whole (Vijayakumar, 2005). This is because people all over the world are turning to nature for peace, happiness and enjoyment. In Africa, 80 per cent of tourists who visited countries in this continent named wildlife as a primary motivational attribute (Filion *et al.*, 1994). Weaver (1998) pointed out that most of the tourists chose the naturally beautiful and unspoiled Third World Countries as their destinations. According to the United Nations World Tourism Organisation (UNWTO), over the past six decades, tourism has experienced continued growth and diversification to become one of the largest and fastest growing economic sectors in the world. It provides jobs to around 260 million people. The international tourist arrivals worldwide grew by 4.4 per cent in 2010 over 2009 (UNWTO, 2012). In 2010 international tourism generated US $ 919 billion in export earnings which is 8 per cent growth over the previous year. The World Travel and Tourism Council (WTTC) estimated that tourism contributed 9.2 per cent of global GDP and forecasts that this will continue to grow at over 4 per cent per annum during the next ten years to account for some 9.4 per cent of Gross Domestic Product (GDP) (WTTC, 2010). Today, for many developing countries, tourism has become the prime source of foreign exchange earnings (Wunder, 1999). It contributes around 10 per cent of the export receipts in India and much more in Nepal and Maldives (Gosslings, 1999). In India tourism plays an important role as a foreign exchange earner for the country. In 2010, India's foreign exchange earnings from tourism were US $ 14.19 billion which increased to US $ 17.74 in 2012 (Indian Tourism Statistics 2012).

At the same time, tourism has a relatively low negative impact on the environment compared to other productive sectors such as agriculture, cattle ranching and mining. With growing global pressures on forest resources and the search for models of sustainable development and sustainable forest use, it has thus been natural to look towards tourism in forest areas as a potential 'win-win' component in the design of conservation strategies and practices (Wunder, 1999). Tourism directed towards natural forests can be viewed as another element within the array of non-timber forest benefits. In principle, as a non-consumptive use of the forest, it is a potentially well-suited element for conservation. In fact, ecotourism is regarded as an alternative to achieve sustainable development. The World Commission on Environment and Development (1987) has named wildlife-based tourism as a desirable component of sustainable development. Ecotourism is considered as a potential means to promote the conservation of biological resources because it has fewer negative impacts on natural resources. However, even non-consumptive ecotourism can have negative environmental impacts such as disturbance to wildlife, impairment of natural scene, soil and vegetation damage. Therefore, there is a need for proper planning and management to minimise negative environmental impacts.

ECOTOURISM POTENTIAL OF ARUNACHAL PRADESH

Arunachal Pradesh, the easternmost State of India, is situated in the Trans-Himalayan region between latitude 26° 28′ N and 29° 33′ N and longitude 91° 31′ E and 97° 30′ E. It is spread over an area 83,743 sq. km. The State is well known for its vast forest resources and rich biodiversity. Due to its geographical location, it falls under Indo-Burma biodiversity 'hotspot' which is one of the mega biodiversity hotspots of the world (Chatterjee *et al.*, 2006). As per the estimate of Forest Survey of India, based on satellite imagery, forest area in this State constitutes around 80.50 per cent of the total are :a of the State, which is one of the highest among the States of North-East India (State of Forest Report, 2011). The important forest species found in the State are tropical, evergreen, semi-evergreen, deciduous, pine, temperate, alpine and grassland. The forest of the State is an important attraction for tourists as it houses diverse species of flora and fauna. Some of the species of plants and animals found in the State are rare and endemic. An analysis reveals that in around 2.5 per cent of India's landmass, the State of Arunachal Pradesh contains nearly 16 per cent of the total timber growing stock of the country and more than 20 per cent of the country's fauna. Moreover, Arunachal Pradesh with its unique geographical position and climate offers excellent growing conditions for orchids. The State is an abode of more than 545 species of orchids which is perhaps the highest number of species of orchids known from any single State of India. It accounts for around 50 per cent of the species of orchids found in the entire country.

In addition, Arunachal Pradesh, 'the land of dawn lit mountains' is blessed with pristine natural beauty. Its landscape is quite fascinating due to uneven topography, dense forest, flora and fauna, river valley, snow covered peaks, passes, crystal natural lakes and cascading waterfalls. Snow falls which occurs during December and January in high altitude tourist spots like Bomdila, Tawang and Mechuka are added attractions to tourists. There are numerous mountain peaks in the State. The most important peaks are Kangto peak (7,090 metres) in West kameng district and Gorichen peak (6,488 metres) in Tawang district. The important passes are Bomdila Pass, Sela Pass, Lumla Pass. The major lakes are Sangetsar Lake and Sela Lake in Tawang district, Ganga Lake in Itanagar, Mehao Lake district and Sally Lake in Lower Dibang valley. The five major rivers of the State are; the Siang river, the Subansiri river, the Kameng river, the Lohit river and the Tirap river. This makes the State an ideal destination for adventure tourism. Adventure activities such as trekking, paragliding, angling, river rafting and boating can be well developed to attract adventure lovers from all over the world.

The State is also highly rich in cultural resources. It is the home of twenty six major tribes and one hundred and ten sub-tribes which is acknowledged to be one of the most splendid and multi-lingual tribal areas of the world. Each tribe in the State has its own tradition, culture and local dialects. Different culture, language, colourful festivals, music and dances of tribal groups are added attractions for tourists.

These facts clearly show that the State has an enormous potential for developing ecotourism as well as adventure tourism. The dense forest and rich biodiversity of the State presents huge opportunities and challenges (Mitra, 2009). The conflict between development process and protecting the biodiversity of the State is becoming increasingly more apparent. Arunachal Pradesh has the unique opportunity to map out a development path that is both sustainable and ecologically sound (Mitra and Lama, 2013). Despite being rich in resource endowment, the State is one of the most backward States of India. In this background, the promotion of tourism appears to be one of the best ways of generating internal revenue, employment, income and accelerating the pace of development in the State. In addition, the promotion of nature-based and ecotourism can play an important role in the State's strategy to conserve the rich forest resources as well as cultural heritage.

However, there needs to be valuation of ecotourism which can help the policy makers to take unbiased decision for proper management and sustainable use of ecotourism resources. Hence, the present study is an attempt to estimate the economic value of ecotourism in Tawang and West Kameng districts of Arunachal Pradesh. These two districts together account for around 60 per cent of the total tourist arrivals in the State, as per the statistics of the Directorate of Tourism, Government of Arunachal Pradesh.

OBJECTIVES OF THE STUDY

The first objective of the study was to study the socio-economic characteristics of the tourists such as gender, age, educational level, nationality, household income and occupation. Secondly, it aims to examine the variables influencing visitation rate and also to estimate the value of ecotourism by estimating the consumer surplus. Thirdly, to calculate the willingness to pay among the tourists for developing adventure tourism. Fourthly, to assess the potential negative impacts of tourism on environment by using the Delphi technique. Finally, to identify the major challenges for the promotion of ecotourism and to suggest measures to overcome those challenges.

HYPOTHESES

The first hypothesis was that the socio-economic characteristics of tourists are expected to influence the visitation rate among the tourists.

Secondly, the socio-economic characteristics of tourists are also expected to influence the willingness to pay.

Thirdly, the value of ecotourism is expected to be high.

METHODOLOGY

The study was an attempt to estimate the value of ecotourism in Tawang and West Kameng districts of Arunachal Pradesh by applying the travel cost method (TCM) and the contingent valuation method (CVM). These two methods have been commonly used to measure the economic value of environmental and non-market goods in developed as well as in developing countries.

The TCM is an indirect method of valuation of environmental goods. This method is most commonly used for assessing the value of national parks meant for preservation of flora and fauna (Chopra, 1998; Hadker *et al.*, 1997). This method values environmental goods on the basis of what people are prepared to pay to travel to them (Clawson and Knetch, 1966). People's travel costs are taken as a surrogate for the price that they pay to visit an environmentally-based attraction and a conventional demand curve is hence established for the non-marked recreation benefit provided. There are two versions of travel cost method (TCM), viz. (1) Individual Travel Cost Method (ITCM) and (2) Zonal Travel Cost Method (ZTCM). ITCM cannot be applied to sites that receive few multiple visits by the same visitors. In such cases, the Zonal Travel Cost Method (ZTCM) is adopted (Tobias and Mendelsohn, 1991). In the present study, the Zonal Travel Cost Method was applied to estimate the recreational value of ecotourism resources because the study area received few multiple visits by the same visitors.

The CVM is a direct method of estimating the non-market value of environmental attributes or amenities such as values of recreational or scenic resources etc. This method is used when markets do not exist for environmental resources (Mitchell and Carson, 1989). The CVM involves the presentation of hypothetical market scenarios to respondents in a survey format, where the scenario involves some trade-off between the amount of a recreational amenity or environmental good and a monetary attribute. This method uses survey to ask the people about their willingness to pay (WTP) for improved environment or willingness to accept (WTA) compensation for damaged environment.

The CVM has been commonly used as one of the standard and flexible approaches to measure the economic values of non-market goods (Hanemann, 1994). This approach is used for valuation of wilderness as well as of common environmental facilities like forests, common lands, common water bodies etc. (Kadekodi *et al.*, 2000). The most appealing aspect of the contingent valuation method is that it allows us to estimate both the use value and non-use values of environmental amenity. It gained popularity after the two major non-use values, namely, option value and existence value. The CVM is the only approach to elicit existence benefits of environment amenity from both users and non-users. There are two approaches to elicit WTP or WTA bids, viz. (i) an open-ended referendum and (ii) a close-ended referendum. A closed-ended format tends to anchor the respondent's answer to a range of values presented. Hence, in the present study an open-ended referendum was applied to elicit tourists' willingness to pay for recreational value of the study area.

The study is mainly empirical in nature and is based on both primary and secondary sources of data. The secondary data used in the study was collected from the Directorate of Tourism, Government of Arunachal Pradesh; Ministry of Tourism, Government of India; and other sources. The primary data was collected by conducting a survey among the tourists in the selected tourist spots in the study area. The survey was based on multi-stage sampling technique. In the first stage two districts namely, Tawang and West Kameng were selected by purposive sampling. In the second stage tourist spots which received the maximum number of tourists were also selected by purposive sampling. Finally, the tourists were selected by random sampling. However, a stratified random sampling technique was used to determine the proportion in which Indian and foreign tourists were selected in the sample. The tourists' survey was conducted during the peak tourist season in the study area. Finally, 309 tourists were interviewed, out of which 278 were domestic tourists and 31 were foreign tourists.

In the sample only those visitors who had a definite source of personal income or family income were selected and interviewed. Proper care was taken in the survey to solve the problem of multi destination visits. The interviews were conducted with the help of a well framed questionnaire to obtain information from the visitors. The questionnaire was subdivided into four sections. Section I of the questionnaire was designed to obtain information about socio-economic characteristics of the tourists. Section II was designed to obtain information relating to travel expenditure, duration of tour, nature and purpose of visit, sources of information, mode of transportation etc. Section III of the questionnaire contained questions to elicit the tourists' maximum willingness to pay for the preservation of the natural environment and for developing adventure tourism. The last section of the questionnaire was formulated to know the tourists' satisfaction level about various facilities enjoyed by them in the study area.

In addition to tourists' survey, a survey was also conducted to generate opinion of experts to assess the potential negative impacts of tourism on environment by applying the Delphi technique. The focal group discussion among local people was also conducted regarding their opinion towards developing tourism in the study area.

BRIEF DESCRIPTION OF THE STUDY AREA

The study was undertaken in the two hilly districts of Arunachal Pradesh namely, West Kameng and Tawang Districts. West Kameng district, which is located in the western corner of the State, is spread over an area of 7,422 sq. km accounting for 8.86 per cent of the total geographical area of the State. The topography of the district is hilly and mountainous as it is located in the eastern Himalayan zone. The total population of the district is 87,013 persons with a population density of 12 persons per sq. km (Provisional Census 2011). The district is inhabited by five major tribes namely, Monpas, Sherdukpens, Mijis, Akas and Buguns. This district has a lot of attraction for the tourists such as its cool climate, vast and varied natural vegetation, lofty mountains, picturesque scenery, river valley, artistic handicrafts and rich culture of the local people. The tourist spots in this district fall under 'The Tezpur-Bhalukpong-Bomdila-Tawang' travel circuit which is one of the eleven travel circuits approved by the Government. The important places of interest in this district are; Bhalukpong, Tipi, Sessa, Bomdila, Dirang and Shergaon.

Bhalukpong is the entry point to West Kameng district. It is famous for archaeological ruins of King Bhaluka, an ancient ruler of the region. It is also known for the mighty Kameng River which passes nearby it in a serene flow and provides a rare opportunity for adventure tourism. Tipi which is located at a distance of 5 km from Bhalukpong is a botanical paradise. It is home to 450 species of orchids, some of which are rare and endangered. There is an orchid museum at Tipi. Natural waterfalls and natural beauty are its added attractions. Sessa is located at a distance of 29 km. from Bhalukpong and is known for a natural orchid sanctuary spread over an area of 10 sq. km.

Bomdila, the Headquarter of the district, is situated at an altitude of 8,500 ft. It is a hill station and is known for cool climate and a picturesque natural beauty of its surroundings. From Bomdila visitors can watch various snow clad mountain peaks including a bird's eye view of Kangto and Gorichen peaks. Dirang which is located at a distance of 42 km from Bomdila is a beautiful valley. It is famous for hot water spring, apple and kiwi orchards, sheep breeding farm and Siberian black neck Storks which visit Sangti valley during winter. Shergaon, which is located at a distance of about 50 km from Bomdila, is famous for the State's largest apple orchard. A trout fish hatchery is also located in periphery of the apple orchard. Its rich natural vegetation and pleasant climate are added attractions for visitors.

Tawang district is located in the north-western corner of the State and shares international boundary with China in the north and Bhutan in the south-west which makes it in a strategic location. The total geographical area of the district is 2,172 sq. km which accounts for 2.59 per cent of the total geographical area of the State. The total population of the district is 49,950 persons with a population density of 23 persons per sq. km (Provisional Census 2011). The district is mainly inhabited by the Monpa tribe of Arunachal Pradesh. The main economic activity of the local people is agriculture and animal rearing (particularly, yak and sheep). Its hilly and mountainous topography has limited cultivable land area which has made the life of the people very hard. However, it is considered as one of the most beautiful place with exotic location and picturesque surroundings. It has a number of beautiful sites such as snow covered mountain peaks, natural lakes, waterfalls, picturesque landscape which provides a breathtaking experience to the visitors. The important places of interest in Tawang districts are; Sela Pass and Sela Lake, Nurannang, Tawang and PTSo Lake.

Sela Pass, situated at an altitude of about 14,000 ft, is the world's second highest motorable pass. A high altitude serene crystal blue natural lake called Sela Lake located adjacent to it is the added attraction to the natural beauty of the surrounding landscape. Nurannang is located at a distance of 12 km. from Sela Pass It is home to cold water snow and rainbow trout fish hatchery and provides an opportunity to visitors to experience fishing in the chilly water. Tawang, the Headquarter of the district, is situated at an altitude of 10,000 ft and is famous for its 400 years old monastery of Mahayana Buddhism called "Galden Namgyel Lhatse", (popularly known as Tawang Monastery) which is the second largest monastery in Asia. Tawang is also famous for its beautiful natural lakes. The most popular lakes are Sangetsar lake, PTSo lake, Sela lake and Bangachanga lake, which have splendid natural beauty. The artistic crafts and rich culture of the local people further add to its beauty making it one of the most attractive destinations for tourists from various parts of the country as well as the world.

These facts clearly show that these two districts have tremendous potential for developing ecotourism. In fact, the development of ecotourism appears to be one of the best options for accelerating the pace of economic development, improving the socio-economic conditions of the local communities as well as for conserving natural environment.

Two

Economic Valuation of Environmental Goods

Review of Literature

Today, the whole world is concerned with the problem of environmental degradation. The largest areas of concern at present are the loss of rain forests, air pollution, ozone depletion and destruction of marine environment. The global concern to protect environment has been manifested in the forms of international environment agreements such as Kyoto Protocol, Vienna convention of the Ozone Layer and Rio Declaration on Development and Environment 1992. Environmental degradation, to a large extent, is the result of market failure or poorly functioning markets for environmental goods and services. Due to absence of market, values of environmental goods are hardly considered in development decisions.

Therefore, economic valuation of environmental goods can play an important role in conservation of environment. Harisson, Bennett and Tisdell (2002) emphasized the need for valuation of non-market values of environmental resources in view of growing demand for them as a result of increasing levels of affluence and education. Economic valuation can serve at least two useful purposes for conservation (Naidoo, 2008). Firstly, valuation can provide information that can directly inform conservation policies. Secondly, valuation studies can be used in general sense to demonstrate that conservation of nature can result in tangible economic benefits to people. The resulting values can either be directly compared to other potential uses of land through cost benefit analysis or can simply serve to raise awareness among policy makers or the general public of the unrecognized economic benefits of conservation. But the valuation of environmental goods is not an easy task due to non-existence of market for such goods. Environmental goods are public goods in nature and cannot be marketed. The absence of a market is the major factor that complicates finding the demand curve for environmental goods. The existence of different kinds of values of environmental goods, further, complicates the economic valuation of such goods.

ECONOMIC VALUE OF ENVIRONMENTAL GOODS

Environmental goods provide a large number of values. These values are basically classified into two categories; (i) use value and (ii) non-use value. Thus, the total economic value of an environmental good constitutes use value and non-use value. An illustration of total value of natural resources is presented in Table 2.1.

Table 2.1: Total Value of Natural Resources

1. Use values		
(i) Direct value	(ii) Indirect value	(iii) Option value
Sustainable timber; Non-timber forest products; Recreation and tourism; Medicine; Plant genetics; Education; Human habitat	Watershed protection Nutrient recycling; Air pollution reduction; Micro-climate functioning; Carbon store; Biodiversity	Future use as per (i) and (ii)
2. Non-use values		
Intrinsic, Existence values: Cultural, religious, and heritage values; Biodiversity		

Source: Pearce and Moran (1995).

Use value is the conventional notion of value associated with the consumption of a good. It is the value derived from actual consumption of a good. In the case of an environmental good, this could include current use, expected use and possible use. Natural resources provide a variety of goods and services to the users from their current or future benefits of welfare. Hence they are said to have use values. Examples of use value includes benefits from use of fuel wood from forests, timbers, minerals from the earth, water from rivers or underground, and non-timber forest products from the forests and so on. The current use of these goods and services can be either direct or indirect. Society also has the option of postponing any decision on the use of any natural resources. Accordingly, the use values can be further broadly classified into three groups; direct use value, indirect use value and option value (Kadekodi, 2001).

Direct use value (DUV) refers to the current use of the resources and economic services provided, directly by natural and biological resources. It can be either consumptive or non-consumptive. Examples are, use of timber and non- timber forest products (NTFPs) and services. Direct consumptive use values from forests include timbers, fuel wood, fodder, medicinal plants, fruits, poles, hunting etc. to the people particularly local communities. Direct non-consumptive values from forests may include ecotourism and recreation (e.g., tourism to wildlife sanctuaries or Himalayan glaciers, mountains), viewing elephants in wild (a case in ecotourism) etc. Mitchell and Carson (1989), Barbier (1994) and Pearce and Moran (1995) regarded recreational use value as direct use value while Bateman (1993) regarded it as indirect use value. Indirect use values (IUV) generally are referred to the ecological functions that natural environment provides us, but without harvesting, depletion or degradation. It can be broadly classified into three groups; watershed values, ecosystem services and evolutionary processes. Watershed values include flood control, regulation of stream flows, recharging of ground water, effect of upstream or downstream, etc.; the ecosystem services include fixing of nitrogen, assimilation of waste, carbon sequestration, gene pool etc.; and evolutionary processes include global live support, religious, cultural and aesthetic concerns, biodiversity preservation, etc.

Non-use values (NUV) are entirely different from use values and are a controversial aspect of value. Non-use value is a value associated with a gain in a person's utility without the person actually using the natural resources. We may value ecosystem in remote parts of the world for reasons other than intending to visit the ecosystem or potentially obtaining something useful from the ecosystem. These values are often revealed through people's perceptions and concerns towards conservation, culture, and aesthetics and so on. Non-use value can be grouped into three categories; Existence Value, Altruistic Value and Bequest Value.

Existence value is the value that individuals may attach to the mere knowledge that rare and diverse species, unique natural environments, or other goods exists, even if these individuals do not contemplate ever making active use of or benefiting in a more direct way from them (Portney, 1994). This would be in addition to any value associated with actual or potential use. Existence value is a concept associated with people's willingness to pay simply for the pleasure they derive from knowing that a natural area is preserved or particular species of flora and fauna are retained irrespective of any plans they may have to hunt, observe or otherwise use these resources (Swanson and Barbier, 1992). People's willingness to pay for the preservation of endangered species is an example of existence value. The potential importance of existence value was shown by Krutilla (1967).

Altruistic value is the value which is derived not from own consumption of environmental goods but from the fact that someone else gains utility. Bequest value is associated with the well being of descendents. If we value passing a wilderness area on to the next generation, that wilderness has a bequest value to us even if we never use it or intend to use it. It refers to the benefits received by retaining the option of using a resource (say, a river basin) in the future by protecting or preserving it today, when its future demand and supply is uncertain.

ECOTOURISM VALUE OF ENVIRONMENTAL GOODS

Ecotourism is one aspect of the numerous values provided by environmental goods. It is the value derived from direct use (non-consumptive use) of the environmental goods such as, forests and natural resources. This includes the benefits derived from recreational activities like tourism and viewing wildlife in natural areas such as, forests, natural reserves and national parks. Ecotourism is dependent on nature environments (both living and non-living) and any indigenous cultures closely connected to such environments (Tisdell, 2001). Ecotourism is a form of nature-based tourism which are non consumptive and mindful of their surrounding environments. Environmental education is an important aspect of ecotourism. Environmental education can release powerful forces to reduce environmental damage. Brandon and Margoluis (1996) noted that the distinguishing feature of ecotourism is that it benefits biodiversity conservation. Ecotourism, which is based on nature and aims to minimize environmental impacts and contribute to economic development of local communities, has shown prospects for successful funding of conservation and sustainable development. Ecotourism can be an effective means of achieving conservation of biological diversity, both for the benefit of tourism and for the economic values of biodiversity.

Tourism is one of the world's largest industries, and is growing rapidly worldwide, particularly in the Asia and Pacific region (28 per cent growth in 2004: WTO, 2006). Ecotourism is an expanding segment of the tourism market. One of the appeals of ecotourism is its potential to provide economic gains in terms of incomes and employment while conserving nature (Tisdell, 1996). Ecotourism depends on minimal impacts to the environment and therefore does not contribute to damaging it. It has come to be recognized as an important tool for promoting sustainable development because it offers the potential of mobilizing resources through the private sector which can contribute to local and national economic development while providing an incentive for conservation of land uses and helping to finance biodiversity conservation.

Economic valuation of ecotourism is necessary to promote conservation and management, to provide a compelling case for intergovernmental efforts to protect the area (Wilson and Tisdell, 2001) and to justify continuing support from the public, government and non-government organizations (Lee and Han, 2002). (Barbier *et al.*, 1997) defines economic valuation as 'an attempt to assign quantitative values to the goods and services provided by environment resources, whether or not market prices are available'. One of the problems in determining the economic value of ecotourism is to know exactly what is meant by the term. A variety of definitions for the term ecotourism, however, the most widely acknowledged definition is given by Ceballos-Lascurian who defines ecotourism as:

> "Tourism that involves travelling to relatively undisturbed natural areas with the specific object of studying, admiring

> and enjoying the scenery and its wild plants and animals as well as any existing cultural aspects (both past and present) found in those areas (Boo, 1990).

This definition of ecotourism was adopted in the study. Because ecotourism resources are not usually traded in a market, non-market valuation techniques are usually applied to estimate their economic value (Upneja *et al.*, 2001). However, the review of the relevant literature reveals that monetary valuation has rarely been used in assessing and evaluating the value of ecotourism. Most of the monetary valuation studies of ecotourism have applied either the travel cost method (Tobias and Mendelsohn, 1991; Maille and Mendelsohn, 1993; Navrud and Mungatan, 1994; Driml, 2002) or the contingent valuation method (Thomas and Hollis, 1991; Lee, 1997; Nuva *et al.*, 2009).

ECONOMIC VALUATION METHODS FOR ENVIRONMENTAL AND NON-MARKET GOODS

Most of the values of natural environmental such as ecosystem function value, recreation value, option value and non-use values (existence value, altruistic value, bequest value) are not accurately known due to non-existence of market price. As a result these values of natural environment are hardly considered in development decision making. Therefore, economists have developed techniques to assess the value of environmental goods. Economic valuation techniques have been developed and used in valuing the environmental goods and services, and are generally known as non-market valuation techniques. Techniques such as the travel cost method to value natural areas for visitors and the contingent valuation method which can both estimate the value for users as well as non-users are being used extensively and are being constantly refined and improved (Moon, 2003). These methods can help economists, governments and society to predict the impact of economic decision and activities on environment and resources and also identify and estimate the monetary value of all economic benefits that a society derives from environmental resources (Nuva *et. al.*, 2009).

The non-market valuation techniques can be broadly divided into two approaches:

I. Revealed Preference Approach and
II. Stated Preference Approach

REVEALED PREFERENCE APPROACH

In revealed preferences approach, we observe a real choice in some market and cleverly infer information on the trade-off between money and the environmental goods. For instance, we may notice that two communities are identical except that one has high housing prices and clean air and the other has lower housing prices and dirty air. We may infer that the difference in housing prices reflects the value that people place on clean air which is an environmental good. Within the category of revealed preference, there are two basic approaches to measuring demand for environmental goods; (i) Hedonic Price Method and (ii) Travel Cost Method. In hedonic approach, the goal is to see how the price of a conventional good (e.g. a house) varies as the amount of a closely related environmental good (e.g. the air quality in the vicinity of the house) changes. This relationship is used to infer the value of environmental goods. On other hand, in travel cost method, the travel cost incurred by the visitors to visit a recreational site is used a proxy for the price paid for recreational experience. One problem in the revealed preference method is that data on market transactions and product characteristics are not readily available.

STATED PREFERENCE APPROACH

The stated preference approach basically involves asking people how much an environmental good is worth. In this approach, opinion polls and surveys are used to derive this information. In the arena of stated preferences, the dominant approach is the contingent valuation method (CVM) which relies on hypothetical market scenario for non-market goods. This method estimates the value of environmental goods by directly asking the people of their willingness to pay (WTP) or willingness to accept compensation (WTAC) for the proposed increase or decrease in environmental quality. The stated preference approach is preferred over the revealed preference approach by economists when the data on market transactions are not reliable or are unavailable.

Travel Cost Method

The travel cost method (TCM) is probably the oldest method of valuing environmental goods. This method was first suggested by Harold Hotelling in 1947 (Garrod and Willis, 1999) and the methodology was subsequently developed in the late 1950s and 1960s by, among others: Trice and Wood (1958); Clawson (1959); and Clawson and Knetsch (1996). This method measures the value of environmental goods (e.g. National park) by observing expenditures incurred to visit the park. People's travel costs are taken as a surrogate for the price that they pay to visit an environmentally-based attraction and a conventional demand curve is hence established for the non-marketed recreation benefit provided. Travel costs would include actual transportation costs, fees paid at hotels and at times the opportunity costs of travel time spent on journey, as proxy for asset value of the recreation site (a non- market asset).

The TCM is most commonly used for assessing the economic use values of ecosystem or sites like national parks meant for preservation of flora and fauna (Chopra, 1998; Hadker *et al.*, 1997). It is typically used to capture the recreational value of sites, such as national parks and sanctuaries. Sometimes, though less often, it has also been applied to problems like finding the value of collected forest products (not routed through the markets) for villagers, by examining the travel and time costs involved in collecting them. In general, the method can be used in situations such as changes in access costs for a recreation site; elimination of an existing recreation site; addition of a new recreation site; changes in environmental quality at a recreational site, etc. (Kadekodi, 2001). This method is widely used to estimate the value of recreational sites such as natural reserves, national parks and sanctuaries.

There are two basic approaches to estimating the demand for a site based on travel cost method; (i) Zonal Travel Cost Method and (ii) Individual Travel Cost Method. The Zonal Travel Cost Method follows directly from the original suggestion of Hotelling. However, the method was applied and developed in detail by Marion Clawson and colleagues at Resources for the Future in the late 1950s and 1960s (Clawson and Knetch, 1966). In this method visitors to a site are divided into different zones of origin. The zones are basically constructed based on distance or political boundary. The only data that need to be collected are a sample of visitors to the site in question, identifying the origin of those visitors' visits. A visitation rate is calculated for each zone by dividing the number of visitors per year from origin zone by the total population of origin zone. This visitation rate is expected to be influenced by the travel cost from the origin zone to the site and the socio-economic characteristics of population of the origin zone. The ZTCM has been widely used to estimate the recreational values of natural areas such as National Parks, reserves and forests since 1960s. The ZTCM is appropriate for sites that have very low individual visitation patterns (Bateman, 1993; Bennett, 1996).

The Individual Travel Cost Method has been successfully applied to a variety of recreational sites since the mid 1980s. In this method, the concept of zoning is absent. Here, the dependent variable is simply the number of visits made by the respondent to the site during a year. Hence, the number of observations in the case of ITCM will be equal to the number of respondents, while in the case of ZTCM, it will be equal to the number of zones. Under ITCM the visitation rate is the total number of visits made by an individual i to the site j. In this method, information is collected on individual visit frequencies over a given time period, information on the cost of travel to the site, recreational preference, use of substitute sites and socio-economic characteristics. These data are used to derive a demand curve from which consumer surplus may be estimated.

However, the travel cost method (TCM) suffers from number limitations. Firstly, the TCM is based on the assumption of identical preferences (Chopra, 2004). It is based on construction of a single demand curve for a large number of individuals. This implies that different individuals are assumed to have identical preference which is unrealistic. Secondly, the TCM also suffers from truncation bias. In this method, data is collected through an on-site survey. As a result, only users are included and non-users are by necessity excluded from the analysis. This leads to truncation bias which may result in faulty consumer surplus estimates. Thirdly, in a travel cost study, value of travel time is considered as an important variable and its exclusion would underestimate the total benefits of travel. However, valuing travel time is difficult one and it has not been conclusively answered (Chopra, 2004). Last but not the least, the TCM can be used to measure only the use value of environmental goods. It cannot be used to estimate the nonuse value of environmental goods which represent a substantial part of the total value of environmental goods.

Despite these limitations, the TCM has been widely used to estimate the recreational and ecotourism value of natural sites such as natural reserves, national parks and natural areas. Many empirical studies have been conducted both in developed and developing countries using the TCM to estimate the recreational value of environmental amenities. For, example, Tobias and Mendelsohn (1991) used the travel cost method (TCM) to measure the value of ecotourism in a tropical rain-forest reserve in Costa Rica. They estimated the ecotourism value of a tropical rain-forest site at Costa Rica – the Monteverde Cloud Forest Biological Reserve (MCFR). The study estimated the ecotourism value in a tropical rainforest in Costa Rica to be around US $ 35 per domestic visit. It was found that domestic recreational visits alone represented an annual value of between US $ 97,500 and US $ 116,200 and foreign visitors represented an additional US $ 400,000 to US $ 500,000 annually, assuming foreign tourists place the same value per trip on MCFR as domestic users do.

Maille and Mandelsohn (1993) also employed the travel cost method to determine the value of ecotourism in a tropical forest reserve in Madagascar. Using the total travel costs of visitors to visit the site, the average consumer surplus per visit for foreign tourist was estimated between $ 276 and $ 360. The study showed that there was a scope for raising the fee substantially from the current fee of $ 11 in light of foreign demand. Navrud and Mungatan (1994) applied both the travel cost method and the contingent valuation methods to estimate the recreational value of wildlife viewing in Lake Nakuru National Park in Kenya. The annual recreational value of wildlife viewing in Lake Nakuru National park was estimated between US $ 7.5 million to US $ 15 million using the Zonal Travel Cost Method (ZTCM). The CVM study gave aggregate annual value of US $ 7.5 million. The study clearly showed that sustainable management of wildlife resources can provide a very significant and much needed revenue source for developing countries in future.

Loewen and Kulshrestha (1995) used the travel cost method

(TCM) and contingent valuation method (CVM) to estimate the economic value of the recreation experience at the Prince Albert National Park (PANP) of Saskatchewan. The result of their study showed that the respondents spent on average $ 30 per person per day on their visit to PANP. The consumer surplus per person per day was estimated to be $ 24 by the TCM and $ 13.68 by CVM. The total recreational value in PANP was estimated at approximately $ 16 million a year.

Menkhaus and Lober (1996) estimated the value of ecotourism of Costa Rica Rainforests for tourists from the USA, using the Monteverde Cloud Forest Reserve as a sample site. The travel cost method was applied and travel expenses were used as a proxy for the value of the park. The consumer surplus was estimated to be approximately US $ 1,150, representing the average annual per person valuation of protected area in Costa Rica. The value for the entire US tourist population who visited Costa Rica's rainforests was estimated to be US $ 68 million. The ecotourism value of Monteverde Cloud Forest Reserve was calculated by multiplying the number of US visitors to Monteverde (17,100) by the average consumer surplus, adjusted for the percentage point of time in Costa Rica that was spent at Monteverde. This resulted in a total annual US ecotourism value of US $ 4.5 million for the Monteverde Reserve.

Herath (1999) estimated the recreational value of Lake Mokoan in Victoria using both the travel cost method and the contingent valuation method. The study found difference between the estimated values in the different variants of the same method. The Zonal Travel Cost Method (ZTCM yielded a consumer surplus of $ 31,363 per year while the Individual Travel Cost Method (ITCM) yielded a consumer surplus of $ 29,000 per year. In case of contingent valuation method, open-ended method provided an estimate of consumer surplus of $ 61,000 and the discrete choice yielded a value of $ 84,000. Curtis (2002) applied the TCM for estimating the demand and value of Salmon angling in Co. Donegal, Ireland. The dependent variable was defined as the number of days taken by an individual in a given period. The demand for Salmon angling was found to be affected by angling quality, age and nationality. The consumer surplus per angler per day was estimated to be approximately IR £ 138.

In a travel cost study, Driml (2002) estimated the consumer surplus for visits to the Wet Tropics of Queensland World Heritage

Area (WTWHA) in North Queensland (an area high in biodiversity values and great scenic beauty). The estimated mean consumer surplus was $ 49 per visitor a day. The total consumer surplus to annual visits by Australian tourists to the WTWHA was estimated between $ 83 M and $ 166 M in 1994 prices (about $ 100 M to $ 200 M in 2002 prices). The study provided a strong support for promoting the effective management of the area to sustain its environmental attractions and maintain the economic benefits to visitors into the place. Chen *et al.* (2004) used travel cost method to estimate the recreational benefits of a beach along the eastern coast of Xiamen Island in China. The total value for the beach and its associated recreation was in excess of US $ 53 million. The study considered the use of entrance fee for the protection of this significant tourism resource.

Mendes and Proenca (2005) made an application of the travel cost method to estimate the recreational value to visitors of ecosystem of the Peneda Geres Nationa Park (PGNP) which is located to North-West of Portugal. Individual version of TCM based on count data models was used to estimate the PGNP's recreation demand function and the subsequent visitor's Marshallian consumer surplus welfare measure and Hicksian consumer surplus. The consumer surplus was estimated to be 123 € per day per visit, and 593 € per each average five days length visit, per visitor. These values suggest that recreation use of nature has a higher value than certain economic activities in the area.

Blackwell (2007) attempted to estimate the recreational value of Mooloolaba beach, Sunshine Coast, Queensland using Individual Travel Cost Method. An attempt was also made to compare the recreational value of the beach visit with other outdoor recreation sites. The cost of travel time was valued at 40 per cent of individual's wage rate. The consumer surplus per person for a recreational day visit to the beach was estimated to be $ 119.95 for the entire sample, $ 107.75 for the visitors and $ 17.41 for the residents. The aggregate annual benefits for recreation day visit at Mooloolaba beach were estimated to be $ 862 million for the entire sample, $ 153 million for residents and $ 205 million for visitors. The beaches visit were found to have higher passive-value than national parks or forests which provided evidence that more attention and resources might be required for beaches.

Contingent Valuation Method

The contingent valuation method is one of the standard approaches for valuing non-marketed resources such as recreation, wildlife, and environmental quality (Hanemann *et al.*, 1991). It is one of the most promising methods and is used when markets do not exist for environmental resources (Mitchell and Carson, 1989). The CVM was originally proposed by Ciriacy-Wantrup in 1947. However, Davis (1963) was the first to use the CVM empirically when he estimated the benefits of goose hunting through a survey among goose hunters (Amirnejad *et al.*, 2006). The CVM became very popular during the 1980s and 1990s for valuing environmental goods. The CVM has also found increased application in supporting government regulatory actions or provision of public goods. In Australia, the government debated whether to preserve or allow mining in an area known as the Kakadu Conservation Zone. In that debate, CV studies played a major role in steering public policy toward preservation (Carson *et al.*, 1994) The principal idea underlying this method is that people have true but hidden preferences for all kinds of ecological goods, and that are capable of transforming these preferences into monetary units. The CVM involves the presentation of hypothetical market scenarios to respondents in a survey format, where the scenario involves some trade-off between the amount of a recreational amenity or environmental good and a monetary attribute. This method uses survey to ask the people about their willingness to pay (WTP) for improved environment or willingness to accept (WTA) compensation for damaged environment. In other words, the CVM measures the value of an environmental good by directly asking the consumers what they would be willing to pay for it, if there were a market.

This approach is used for valuation of wilderness as well as of common environmental facilities like forests, common lands, common water bodies etc. (Kadekodi *et al.*, 2000). It gained popularity after the two major non-use values, namely, option value and existence value. The CVM is the only approach to elicit existence benefits of environment amenity from both users and non-users. However, the CVM is subject to controversy because of the absence of real choices, as only the real choices involve actual trades between money and environmental goods. It suffers from several biases like hypothetical bias, strategic bias and embedding bias.

Despite these biases, many empirical studies have applied the contingent valuation method to estimate the recreational value of natural environment such as natural reserves, forests in developed as well in India developing countries. For example, Haefele *et al.* (1991) reported a positive WTP for protecting high-elevation spruce-fir forests in the southern Appalachain Mountains from exotic insect infestations and air pollution damages. Using a decomposition approach, they found that non-use values (bequest and existence values) dominated use values as reasons for protecting these forests. Thomas and Hollis (1991) estimated the annual revenue generated by entry fees charges to visitors of the Ichkeul National Park (INP), Tunisia to be 23, 247 TD. The study showed the total economic value (actual use-value, existence value and option value) of the Ichkeul National Park to be much higher providing adequate justification for taking measures to prevent degradation of the wetland of the park.

Fatley and Bennett (1996) used contingent valuation method to estimate the conservation value of two rainforest areas in the Republic of Vanautu. The study found that Australian tourists visiting Vanautu by international airline would be willing to pay (WTP) around $ 40,3000 per annum to preserve two areas of tropical rain forest on the Islands of Malakula and Erromango and a valuation of approximately $ 20 per Australian visitor to Vanautu. Von Buren *et al.* (1996) used contingent valuation method to estimate the recreational values of salmon and herring fishing in Western Australia. The mean individual willingness to pay (WTP) was estimated to be $ 27.36 per year and an aggregate WTP was estimated to be $ 2.85 million per year.

Lee (1997) attempted to measure the potential revenue from nature-based tourism resources in the environmentally sensitive area of Mt. Minju, South Korea. A dichotomous contingent valuation method was employed to estimate the mean willingness to pay, contingent on a hypothetical markets scenario. The economic value of nature based tourism was estimated at 5905 Won (US $ 7) per visitor. Duthy (2002) applied contingent valuation method to examine whether the Whian Whian State Forest in north-east New South Wales (a remnant of the 'big scrub' area of high ecological values) should be converted to a National

Park. The study explored the various components of the community value, hence shedding light on why people feel strongly about forests conservation area. The mean willingness to pay of respondents for the non-consumptive uses and non-use values of Whian Whian State Forest was $ 18.89 per annum for three years.

Ly *et al.* (2006) applied contingent valuation method to estimate the WTP of recreational visitors to the Djoudj National Bird Park (DNBP) in northern Senegal. Both the open-ended and closed-ended question formats to elicit WTP of the visitors. The findings of their study suggested that the price of visitor admission to the DNBP could be increased substantially from the current official price of 2000 FCFA (about 3 Euros) per person, in line with the WTP expressed by visitors. Togridou *et al.* (2006) examined the importance of visitors' profile, information sources, environmental dispositions and visit evaluation on visitors willingness to pay (WTP) for conservation of the National Marine Park of Zakynthos, Greece (NMPZ). The mean WTP was estimated to be 6.15 Euro. Taking account a rough estimate of 350,000 tourists visiting the park on an annual basis as well as the percentage of the sample that agreed to the payment principle question, the annual revenue was estimated to be 300,000 Euro to 1,400,000 Euro which could cover the operating costs of the Protected Area Management Body.

Sattout *et al.* (2007) applied contingent valuation method to obtain the willingness to pay of Lebanese population to conserve cedal forests in Lebanon. Open-ended questionnaire was used to elicit the willingness to pay. The mean annual WTP per household for the users was found to be approximately US $ 20 which was greater than that for the non-users in both the cases. The mean annual WTP for the total sample (cities and villages) was estimated to be US $ 42.43 per household.

Baral, Stern and Bhattarai (2008) administered a contingent valuation survey to 315 foreign visitors to the Annapurna conservation area, Nepal during April and May 2006 to determine their willingness to pay entry fees. Their objective was to examine possibility of enhancing Annapurna Conservation Area's revenues through increasing tourist entry fees to the area. Most visitors were found willing to pay an entry fee considerably higher than the current fee of US $ 27. The mean and median WTP were US $ 69.2

and US $ 74.3 respectively. The most common explanation for WTP by respondents was a desire to better protect the environment. Based on findings, the study recommended an increase in the entry fee to US $ 50. The important determinants of WTP were; family size, visitor's satisfaction, the use of a guide and group size. The local economic impact from ecotourism was estimated to be a per capita net average annual income of approximately US $ 60 amongst the 120,000 residents of the region.

Using the contingent valuation method, Jin *et al.* (2008) attempted to examine the public willingness to pay for black-faced Spoonbill conservation in Macao. The study also made an attempt to investigate the potential effect of payment vehicles under a mandatory surcharge and a voluntary payment using a split sample. The mean WTP of households for black-faced Spoonbill conservation in Macao ranged from US $ 2.25 to US $ 4.82 per household per month in five years depending on payment schemes. They found a statistically significant difference in WTP responses in two different payment schemes. Mandatory payment mechanism yielded a higher WTP than voluntary payment mechanism. Based on this finding they inferred that the payment vehicle was important in eliciting WTP. The conservation values of black-faced Spoonbill in Macao ranged between US $ 16 million to US $ 34 million for a period of five years.

Nuva *et al.* (2009) also employed contingent valuation method to determine the visitors' WTP for conservation of the ecotourism resources at Gunung Gede Pangrango National Park (TNGP), West Java, Indonesia. The mean WTP was estimated to be RP 7629.77 per visit. The benefit of conservation of the ecotourism resources in TNGP amounted to RP. 452 million in 2004. Ezebilo *et al.* (2010) applied the contingent valuation method to estimate community willingness to contribute for an ecotourism project and its determinants in the Okwangwo Division of the Cross River National Park, Nigeria. The mean willingness to contribute (MWTC) of the respondents was estimated to be NGN 1,047. The MWTC for male (NGN 1,215) was found to be higher than that for female (NGN 885). The willingness to pay was influenced by factors such as income, distance, post-high school education, occupation and membership of an environmental conservation group.

ENVIRONMENTAL VALUATION STUDIES IN INDIA AND NORTH-EAST INDIA

In India as well as in North-East India only a few studies have been undertaken so far to estimate the economic value of environmental amenities. The most important study in India is the economic valuation of biodiversity in Keoladeo National Park, Bharatpur by Chopra *et al.* (1997) using two alternative methodologies viz., travel cost method and an ecological economics inspired multi-criteria approach. Chopra (1998) applied a version of travel cost method to determine the value of tourism and the nature of demand for it in a study of Keoladeo National Park of Rajasthan. The data were collected regarding tourists' travel and stay expenses, duration of stay and various social-economic characteristics. The total number of tourists covered in this study were 305, consisting of 235 Indian and 70 foreign tourists. Using the TCM, the consumer surpluses enjoyed by the domestic and foreign tourists were estimated to be around ₹ 427.04 and ₹ 432 per visit respectively. The study suggested that biodiversity conservation could be more effective way of generating economic benefits and conservation if stakeholders are involved in a meaningful way in the management of the park.

Hadker, Sharma, David and Muraleedharan (1997) surveyed the residents of Mumbai to elicit their willingness to pay for the maintenance and preservation of Borivli National Park (BNP) which is a home to a large number of endangered mammals, birds and reptiles and is one of the most popular parks in India. The households were found to be willing to pay, exclusively for BNP, on an average of ₹ 7.5 per month for the next five years. This amounted to a substantial of ₹ 20 million each month for the next five years on extrapolating to the city Mumbai. The findings suggested a strong interest of the people in environmental conservation. Manoharan and Dutt (1999) used the contingent valuation method to estimate the value of ecotourism resources at Kalakade Mundanthurai Tiger Reserve, Tamil Nadu. The annual value of ecotourism in the reserve was estimated to be ₹ 2.95 million (₹ 34.68 per visitor).

Using the travel cost method, Singh and Gopal (2002) estimated the recreational value of the Lake Nainital, Uttarakhand. The recreational value of the lake was estimated to be ₹ 4.3 million to

₹ 6.5 million. Haque (2003) applied the travel cost method to estimate the economic value of Indian Sundarbans, West Bengal. The consumer surplus derived by the tourists visiting the Sundarbans was estimated to be ₹ 624 per person per visit. Bulov and Lundgren (2007) also applied the travel cost method to estimate the recreational value of Periyar National Park (PNP), Kerala. The total consumer surplus enjoyed by the visitors to the park was estimated to be US $ 15 billion annually.

Guha and Ghosh (2009) applied the travel cost method (TCM) to estimate the recreational demand for the Indian Sundarban, a world heritage site and a complex mangrove ecosystem. Based on Zonal Travel Cost Method (ZTCM), the annual recreational value (in terms of consumer surplus) of the Indian Sundarban as estimated to be approximately ₹ 15 million (US $ 377,000), taking 63,900 visitors during 2005-06. The current entry fee to visit the Sundarban was observed to be very low and park authorities were able to capture less than 10 per cent of consumer surplus. The study estimated that if the fees were increased from the current value of ₹ 15 to ₹ 154 per visitor per day, total revenue could be increased by more than 300 per cent which would bring nearly ₹ 5 million (US $ 0.12 million) per year in revenue to the park.

In North-East India, very few studies have been undertaken to measure the recreational use value of environmental goods. Mitra (2000) possibly for the first time applied the travel cost method to estimate the recreational value of environmental amenities in some selected tourist spots in Arunachal Pradesh. The study derived the demand curve for tourism in Arunachal Pradesh and also estimated the consumer surplus enjoyed by the domestic and foreign tourists. The consumer surpluses enjoyed per person per visit by the domestic and foreign tourist were estimated to be ₹ 991.51 and ₹ 1232.48 respectively and the total consumer surplus was estimated to be ₹ 6.96 million annually. However, the study relied only on the travel cost method and at that time tourist arrival in the State was very low.

Maharana *et al.* (2000) applied both the travel cost method and the contingent valuation method (CVM) to assess the recreational, biodiversity and sacredness values of Khecheopalri Lake, Sikkim. The demand function for recreation was observed to increase with decrease in travel cost and distance for Sikkimese visitors. The travel cost model using the local pilgrims' response put the sacredness value at US $ 30,186. The consumer surplus for visits to Khecheopalri Lake was estimated to be US $ 661 for domestic tourists and US $ 1562 for foreign tourists. The recreational value of the lake was observed to be similar to the other protected sites in India. The annual willingness to pay for maintenance and preservation of the lake by all types of visitors was estimated to be US $ 0.88 for members of the local community, US $ 2.16 for local pilgrims, US $ 2.51 for resident visitors and US $ 7.19 for international tourists. The aggregate WTP for Khecheopalri Lake was estimated to be US $ 46,940 for the maintenance and preservation of the lake based on the total visitors per year. The study revealed that a large number of lakes in the Hindu-Kush Himalayan region, if properly managed and marketed for ecotourism, can bring economic development that can be linked with conservation.

Bhandari (2008) assessed the tourist's willingness to pay for nature-based tourism and biodiversity conservation in Sikkim. The mean WTP of domestic and foreign tourists was estimated at ₹ 73 and ₹ 68.8 respectively. This represented the tourists' WTP to improve biodiversity conservation. Das (2010) applied both the travel cost method and contingent valuation method to estimate ecotourism value of Manas National Park, Assam. The Zonal Travel Cost Method was used to derive demand function and to estimate consumer surplus and open-ended approach of the CVM was used to elicit tourists' willingness to pay (WTP) for conservation of the park. The consumer surplus was estimated to be ₹ 6203.05 per visit for the tourists. The mean WTP was estimated to be ₹ 369.16 for domestic tourists and ₹ 2235.42 for foreign tourists.

De and Devi (2011) studied the impact of various social, economic and locational factors on the visiting decision of the tourists to Cherrapunjee in Meghalaya. The recreational benefit enjoyed by the visitors was estimated by applying both the travel cost method and contingent valuation method. The distance travelled and travel cost incurred by the visitors was found to have significantly negative impacts on the frequency of visit, while income and education had significantly positive impacts on the same.

Thus, we find that in spite of the fact that the North Eastern

Region of India is a biodiversity hotspot and rich in forest resources and natural attraction only a few studies have been undertaken to estimate the recreational and ecotourism value of natural environment. The valuation studies are important as they influence the development decision making process in favour of conservation of environment. Hence, the present study made an attempt to fill this gap in knowledge. The study would also serve as a guide to the policy makers in taking unbiased decision for sustainable management of natural environment.

Three

Socio-Economic Profile of the Tourists

The study of socio-economic characteristics of tourists is considered important in any recreational demand study: This is because the demand for recreation to a great extent is influenced by visitors' socio-economic characteristics. Since the present study attempted to calculate the visitation rate and examined the factors influencing it, it was felt pertinent to study the socio-economic profile of the tourists surveyed. The study of the socio-economic profile of the visitors includes age, gender, educational qualification, primary occupation, annual household income, etc. The study of such characteristics of the tourists is considered necessary for ensuring promotion of ecotourism in a sustainable manner in fragile natural areas and our study area belongs to such type of natural areas.

The data of the socio-economic background was obtained through survey and interview of the tourists. The section one of the questionnaire was designed to obtain information on socio-economic characteristics such as, age, gender, educational level, primary occupation and monthly and annual household income.

CLASSIFICATION OF SURVEYED TOURISTS

Nationality and Gender

In order to obtain date on socio-economic background of the tourists, field surveys were conducted during the peak tourist seasons and tourists stationed at hotels and lodges were interviewed. A total of 309 tourists were surveyed and interviewed. Out of the total tourists surveyed, 89.97 per cent were domestic tourists and rest 10.03 per cent were foreign tourists. An analysis of gender-wise distribution of the surveyed tourists revealed that 80.26 per cent were male and 19.74 per cent were female. Among the surveyed domestic tourists 82.73 per cent were male and only 17.27 were female. While among the surveyed foreign tourists 58.06 per cent were male and 41.94 per cent were female. Thus, it was found that female consisted of a good proportion among the foreign tourists. So it can be inferred that foreign female tourists have better mobility than their domestic counterparts so far as Arunachal visit is concerned.

State of Origin

The surveyed domestic tourists were further, classified on the basis of their State of origin. This exercise was carried out to know the sources of demand for recreation/ecotourism in the study area and to calculate visitation rate on the basis of State or zone. From the survey, it was found that the tourists came to visit Arunachal Pradesh from almost all the States of India. However, it was found that majority of them were from West Bengal (57.91%), followed by Maharashtra (10.43%), Assam (10.07%), New Delhi (2.52%) Rajasthan (2.52%) and Gujarat (2.16%). The details are given in Figure 3.1. It was surprising to know that tourists from North Eastern States other than Assam consisted of only 1.44 per cent among the surveyed domestic tourists.

It was observed that most of the visitors were basically from plain States. They were visiting in large proportion mainly to enjoy mountainous natural beauty, experience pleasant climatic condition, snowfall and to understand the tribal life and their culture.

Country of Origin

The surveyed foreign tourists were classified on the basis of country of origin. From the survey, it was found that majority of the surveyed foreign tourists were from the USA (29.03%), followed by UK (25.81%), Italy (16.13%) and Germany (9.68%). The details are given in Figure 3.2.

It was surprising to know that among the surveyed foreign tourists there was not a single tourist from the Asian countries.

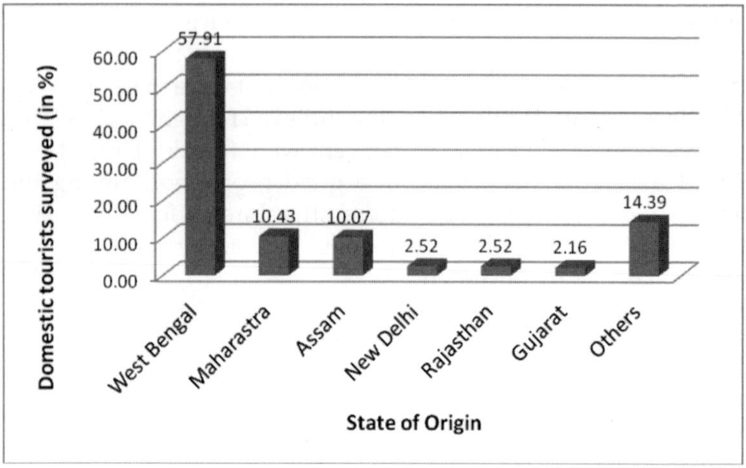

Source: Survey Data, 2009-2011
Figure 3.1: Domestic Tourists Classified by State of Origin

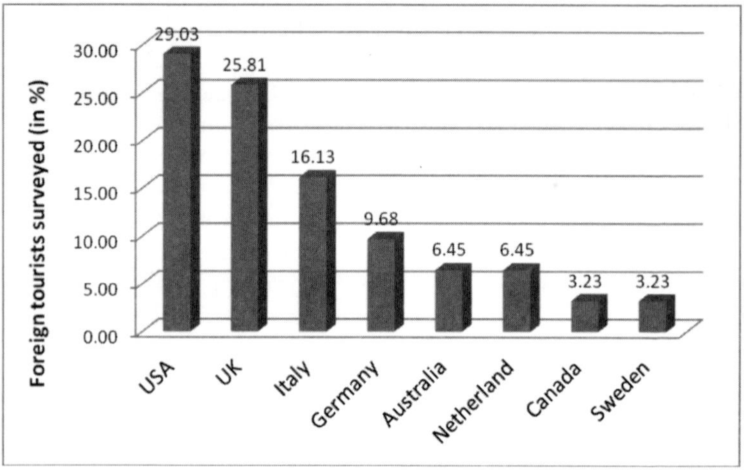

Source: Survey Data, 2009-2011
Figure 3.2: Foreign Tourists Classified by Country of Origin

Age Group

In the recreational demand study, age of the visitor is regarded as one of the important factors determining the demand for recreation. In this study, age was also taken as one of the factors influencing the visitation rate. So an attempt was made to study the age profile of the surveyed tourists. For this purpose, the surveyed tourists were classified into different age groups to examine the proportion of tourists in each age group.

It was found that 7.77 per cent of the surveyed tourists were in the age group of below 25 years, 20.06 per cent were in the age group of 25-35 years, and 22.01 per cent were in the age group of 35-45 years, 29. 13 per cent were in the age group of 45-60 years, remaining 21.04 per cent were in the age group of 60 years and above.

Out of total tourists surveyed slightly more than 50 per cent belonged to the age group within 45 years and they may be regarded as young and enthusiastic. The study of the age profile of the surveyed domestic and foreign tourists separately revealed that a good proportion of surveyed domestic tourists (28.42%) were in the age group of 45-60 years followed by 24.10 per cent in the age group of 35-45 years (Figure 3.3). The average age of the surveyed domestic tourists was calculated to be 41.17 years. On the other hand, it was surprising to note that most of the surveyed foreign tourists (51.61%) were in the age group of 60 years and above followed by 35.48 per cent in the age group of 45-60 years (Figure 3.4). The average age of the surveyed foreign tourists was calculated to be high i.e. 53.43 years.

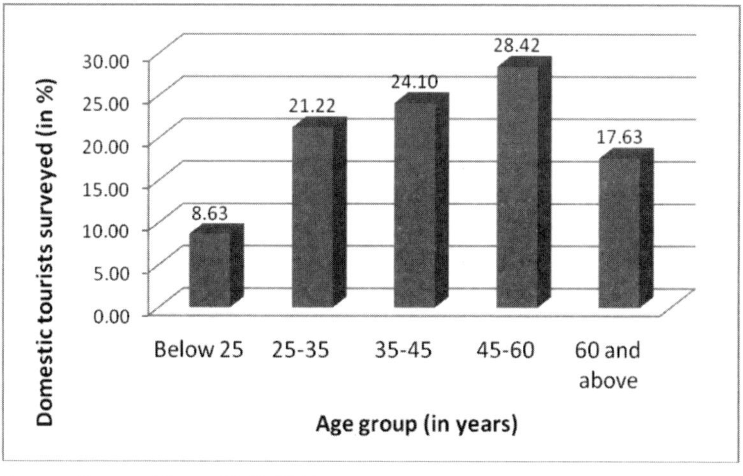

Source: Survey Data, 2009-2011.
Figure 3.3: Classification of Domestic Tourists by Age Group

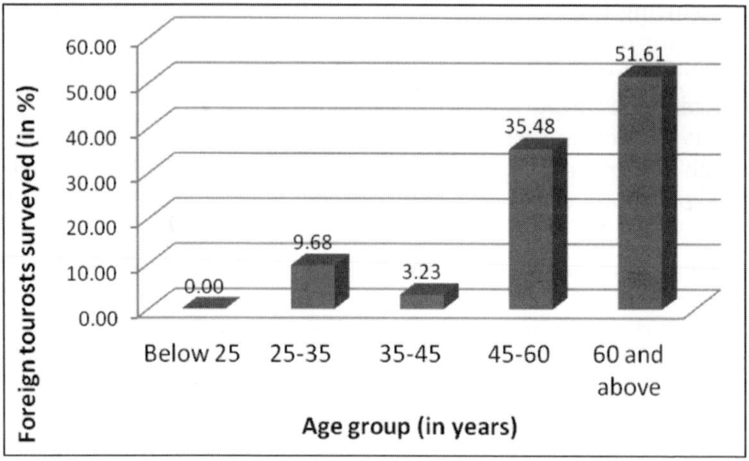

Source: Survey Data, 2009-2011.
Figure 3.4: Classification of Foreign Tourists by Age Group

Thus, it was observed that 45.32 per cent of the surveyed domestic tourists belonged to relatively young age group. On the other hand, majority of the surveyed foreign tourists (51.61%) belonged to the old age group (60 years and above). This may be due to the fact that most of the surveyed foreign tourists were retired employees who had much leisure time to travel for recreation and for whom the opportunity cost of time was comparatively less.

Educational Level

In recreational demand analysis educational attainment is considered as an important factor influencing the visitation rate. Hence, an attempt was made to assess the educational profile of the tourists. It was found that most of the tourists surveyed were sufficiently educated. None of them was reported to be illiterate. Majority of the surveyed tourists were graduates (51.13%) followed by post graduates and above (31.83%). Among the surveyed tourists, 6.80 per cent were educated up to higher secondary and 2.91 per cent were educated up to secondary level. Only 0.31 per cent of the surveyed tourists were educated up to primary level.

Among the surveyed domestic tourists, majority of them were graduates (55.04%) followed by post graduates and above (34.17%), higher secondary level (7.20%), secondary level (3.24%) and primary level (only 0.36%) (Figure 3.5).

In the case of foreign tourists surveyed, majority of them were highly educated. It was found that a very high percentage of the surveyed foreign tourists (80.65%) were post graduates and above followed by graduates (16.13%) and higher secondary level (3.23%) (Figure 3.6).

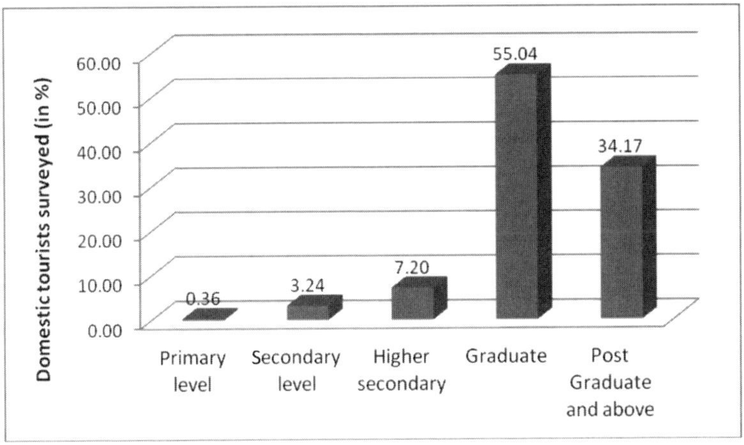

Source: Survey Data, 2009-2011.

Figure 3.5: Domestic Tourists Classified by Education Level

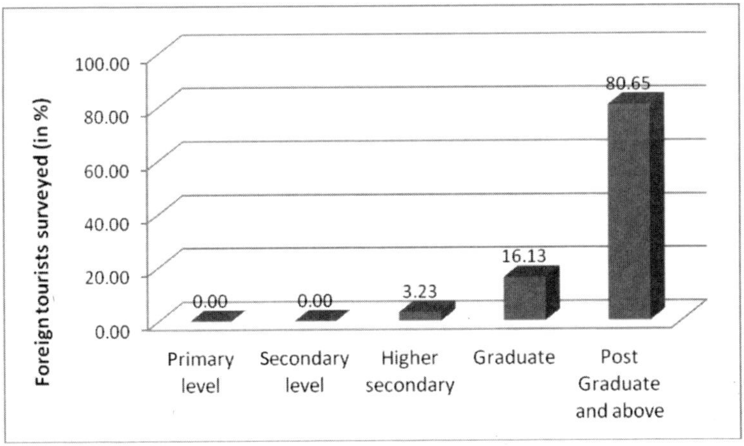

Source: Survey Data, 2009-2011.

Figure 3.6: Foreign Tourists Classified by Educational Level

Occupation

Tourists surveyed were also classified on the basis of primary occupation. This was done to know dominance of visitors from different categories of occupation. During the survey tourists were asked to indicate their occupation category. The question on occupation of the tourists contained four occupation categories, namely, (i) salaried employee (Government/private), (ii) self-employed (business/trade), (iii) professional/consultant and (iv) any other. The analysis of data showed that most of the surveyed tourists were salaried employee (54.37%), followed by self-employed and business (15.86%). The rest of the surveyed tourist belonged professional/consultant (14.24%) and any other category (15.53%). Any other category included mostly social workers, members of NGOs, writers, housewife etc.

The study of the occupational category of the surveyed domestic and foreign tourists revealed that most of the domestic tourists were salaried employee (55.40%) followed by self-employed (16.91%), any other (15.47%) and professional/ consultant (12. 23%) (Figure 3.7). In the case of surveyed foreign tourists also, most of them were salaried employee (45.16%). However, a good percentage of the surveyed foreign tourists (32.26%) were found to be professional/consultant. A good number

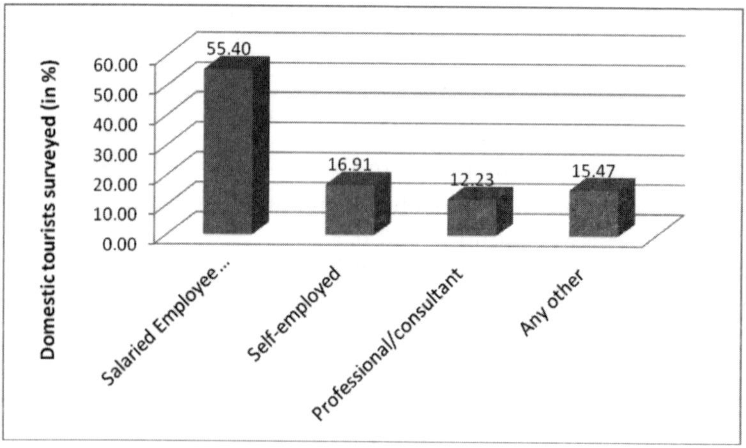

Source: Survey Data, 2009-2011.
Figure 3.7: Domestic Tourists Classified by Occupation

of the surveyed foreign tourists in the salaried category were found to be pensioners (Figure 3.8).

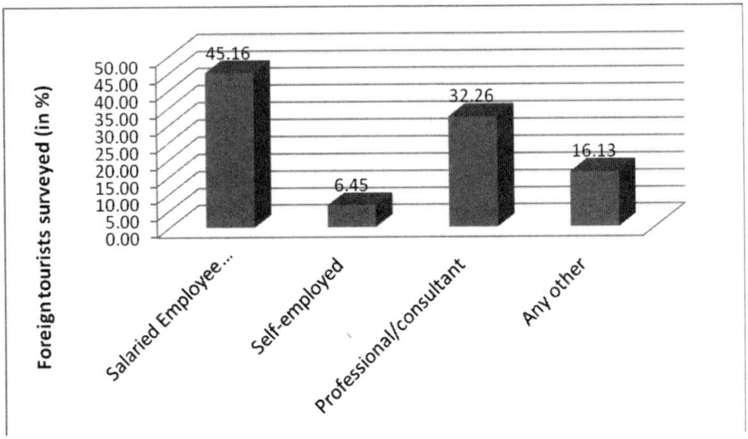

Source: Survey Data, 2009-2011.
Figure 3.8: Foreign Tourists Classified by Occupation

Annual Household Income

The visitor's income is considered to be one of most important factors influencing the demand for recreation in any site or destination. However, during the survey most of the tourists were reluctant to reveal their actual amount of income. It was observed that majority of the surveyed domestic tourists (52.17%) were having annual household income of more than ₹ 5 lakhs. In fact, around 18 per cent of the surveyed domestic tourists had an annual household income of more than ₹ 10 lakhs (Figure 3.9).

The average annual household income of the surveyed domestic tourists was found to be ₹ 6,30,275. On the other hand, as expected most of the surveyed foreign tourists belonged to a very high income category. It was found that 67.74 per cent of the surveyed foreign tourists were having annual household income of ₹ 50 lakhs and above followed by 16.13 per cent in between ₹ 20-30 lakhs (Figure 3.10). The average annual household income of the surveyed foreign tourists was found to be ₹ 60,29,032.

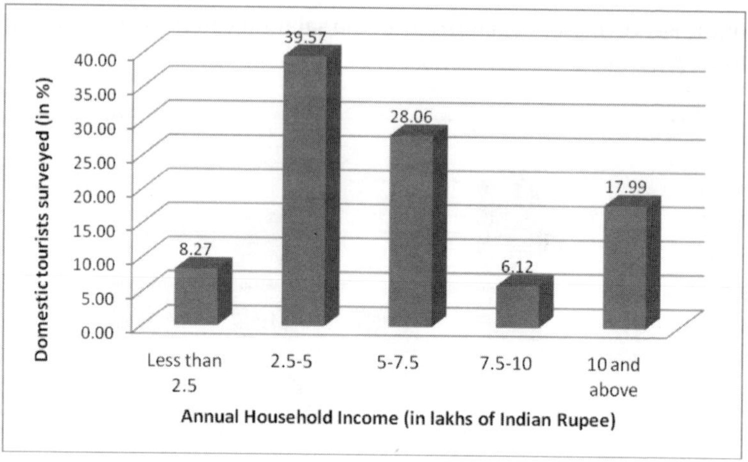

Source: Survey Data, 2009-2011.

Figure 3.9: Domestic Tourists Classified by Annual Household Income

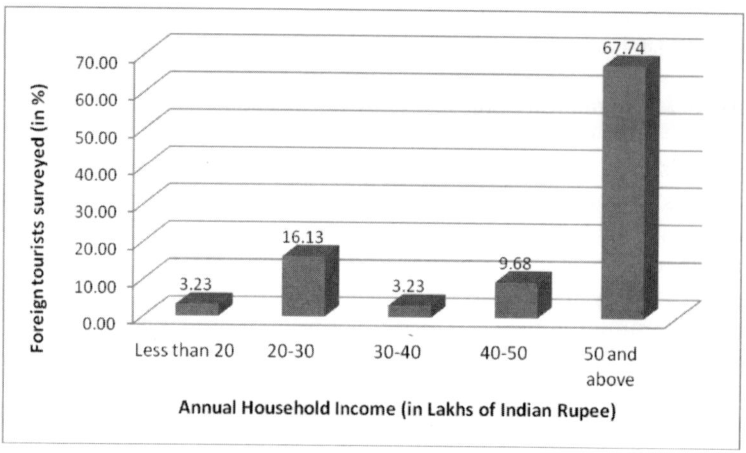

Source: Survey Data, 2009-2011.

Figure 3.10: Foreign Tourists Classified by Annual Household Income

Different Groups

From the survey, it was found that most of the surveyed domestic tourists (81.65%) were family oriented. Either they travelled with their own family members (48.92%) or they travelled in a group of more than one family (32.73%). Only a few surveyed domestic tourists (4.32%) travelled alone (Table 3.1).

In the case of surveyed foreign tourists also a good percentage (38.71%) of them preferred to travel with their own family members (basically couple). It was found that 25. 81 per cent of the surveyed foreign were travelling in a group of friends without family and 16.13 per cent travelled as a single person (Table 3.1).

Table 3.1: Tourists Classified by Different Groups

Type of Group	*Domestic (%)*	*Foreign (%)*
As a single person	4.32	16.13
With own family members	48.92	38.71
In a group of more than one family	32.73	6.45
In a group of friends without family	11.51	25.81
Not specified	2.52	12.9

Source: Survey Data, 2009-2011.

Number of Visiting Members

The visitors were also asked to mention the number of members travelling in their group. The details are presented in Table 3.2.

Table 3.2: Tourists Classified by Number of Visiting Members

Visiting Members	*Domestic (%)*	*Foreign (%)*
Single	4.32	16.13
Two	12.59	58.06
Three	22.3	12.9
Four	13.31	3.23
Five	8.99	6.45
Six	11.51	3.23
More than six	26.98	0

Source: Survey Data, 2009-2011.

It was found that a good percentage of the surveyed domestic tourists (26.98%) were travelling in a group of more than six members followed by 22.30 per cent in a group of three members. It was found that 48.20 per cent of surveyed domestic tourists were found to be travelling in a group consisting of two, three and four members (basically with own family members).

However, among the surveyed foreign tourists majority of them (58.06%) came in a group of two. It can be assumed that a significant percentage of foreign tourists came as a couple. At the same time, 16.13 per cent of surveyed foreign tourists came alone.

Source of Information

An attempt was also made to know the main sources of information about tourist spots in the State. This was considered important due to the remoteness of the area and limited source of information available about the State. The responses of the surveyed tourists are presented in Table 3.3.

Table 3.3: Sources of Information to Tourists about Tourists Spots

Source	*Domestic (%)*	*Foreign (%)*	*Total (%)*
Print media	31.3	16.13	30.04
Television	8.63	0	7.77
Internet	23.02	54.84	26.21
Word of mouth	28.78	12.9	27.18
From previous visit	6.12	6.45	6.15
Any other source	2.16	9.68	2.91

Source: Survey Data, 2009-2011

The Table 3.3 shows that most of the surveyed domestic tourists (31.30%) came to know about the Study area through print media (newspapers, brochures and magazines) followed by word of mouth (28.78%) and internet (23.02%). Those who indicated any other source informed that they came to know about the study area through travel agent and official sources (Table 3.3).

On the other hand, for majority of the surveyed foreign tourists (54.84%) internet was the main source of information followed by print media (16.13%).

Type of Tour Performed

It was found that majority of the surveyed tourists (58.90%) visited on a self-arranged tour and the rest 41.10 per cent visited on a package tour. The study of type of tour performed by surveyed domestic and foreign tourists showed that majority of the surveyed tourists (both domestic and foreign) visited on a self- arranged tour. Among the surveyed domestic tourists 58.63 per cent visited on a self-arranged tour, while among the foreign tourists 61.29 per cent visited on self-arranged tour.

FREQUENCY OF VISIT AMONG SURVEYED TOURISTS

The information on frequency of visit of tourists is important to calculate their visitation rate. So, an attempt was made to collect information on frequency of visit of the surveyed tourists in the study area. From the survey, it was found that most of the surveyed tourists (87.70%) were visiting in the study area for the first time and the rest 12.30 per cent visited more than once (Table 3.4). It was interesting to note that 25.80 per cent of the surveyed foreign tourists visited the study area more than once.

Table 3.4: Frequency of Visit among the Tourists

Frequency of Visit	*Domestic (%)*	*Foreign (%)*	*Total (%)*
First Visit	89.21	74.2	87.7
More than once	10.79	25.8	12.3
Total	100	100	100

Source: Survey Data, 2009-2011.

RESPONSE OF SURVEYED TOURISTS ON FACILITIES ENJOYED

The main motive of the tourists in visiting a place or a site is to derive maximum utility from recreation. The maximization of utility of tourists depends on a number of factors such as physical and social attributes of the site (landscape, scenery, climate, natural beauty, art and crafts, attitude of local people) as well as facilities available (accommodation, transportation, food and beverages, servicing standard etc.) at the tourist destination. In this section an attempt was made to examine the tourists' satisfaction level from the facilities enjoyed in the study area. The suggestions made by the surveyed tourists relating to improving existing facilities were also incorporated. During the survey tourists were asked to rank the facilities available (accommodation, food and beverages, transportation) into three categories i.e. good, moderate and need to improve. The responses of the domestic and foreign tourists surveyed are presented in Table 3.5 and Table 3.6.

The analysis of data showed that majority of the surveyed domestic tourists (43.90%) was satisfied with accommodation facilities. Their responses were either good or moderate as far as the accommodation facilities were concerned. However, a good

Table 3.5: Responses of Domestic Tourists on the Facilities Enjoyed

(in percentage)

Facilities	*Good*	*Moderate*	*Need to Improve*
Accommodation	43.9	27	9.1
Food Quality	29.1	41	29.9
Transportation	14	13.3	72.7

Source: Survey Data, 2009-2011.

Table 3.6: Responses of Foreign Tourists on the Facilities Enjoyed

(in percentage)

Facilities	*Good*	*Moderate*	*Need to Improve*
Accommodation	29	35.5	35.5
Food Quality	35.5	51.6	12.9
Transportation	29	29	42

Source: Survey Data, 2009-2011.

percentage of surveyed foreign tourists (35.50%) opined for the improvement of accommodation facilities. As far as quality of food was concerned, majority of the surveyed foreign tourists were satisfied. However, a good percentage of surveyed domestic tourists (29.90%) were of opinion that it needed to be improved.

Easy and safe accessibility to a tourist destination is also an important factor determining the demand for recreation in that site. Hence, an attempt was made to examine tourists' perception about the mode of transportation as well as condition of roads in the study area. It was found that irrespective of domestic and foreign tourists, most of the surveyed tourists were not at all satisfied with condition of roads and transport facilities and suggested for its improvement. 72.70 per cent of surveyed domestic tourists and 42 per cent of surveyed foreign tourists suggested for improving transport and road condition (Table 3.5 and Table 3.6). In fact, a good number of surveyed tourists opined in their interview that the first and the foremost requirement were to improve transport facilities and road condition for development of tourism in the State.

However, despite poor road condition and absence of better means of transport and other facilities, a very high percentage of the surveyed tourists (95.15%) were willing to visit the State again.

Those who were willing to visit again, however, suggested for improving condition of roads which is the only means of transport to visit the tourist spots in the study area. The analyses of data for domestic and foreign tourists showed that majority of both the categories of the surveyed tourists were willing to visit the State again. It was found that 95.33 per cent of the surveyed domestic tourists and 93.50 per cent of the surveyed foreign tourists expressed their willingness to visit the State again. At the same time a very high percentage of the surveyed tourists (96.12%) expressed desire to share their experience of visiting the State with their friends and relatives and advice them for visiting the State. A very high percentage of the surveyed domestic tourists (96.40%) and foreign tourists (93.50%) stated that they would advice their friends and relatives to visit tourist spots in the study area.

The above analysis and discussion clearly shows that tourists visit the study area mainly to enjoy its pristine natural beauty. The study of socio-economic characteristics of the tourists revealed that around half of the surveyed tourists were young and a good percentage of them were interested in adventure activities. Hence, building of facilities for adventure activities and organizing of such activities can attract more youthful tourists which may boost local economy. Most of the surveyed tourists, particularly domestic tourists, were salaried employees who were travelling with their families. They mostly preferred better facilities at reasonable price. It was found that a good number of the surveyed foreign tourists desired to avail home stay facilities, since they were more interested to know local people and their culture. Hence, it calls for promoting home-stay model as will directly benefit the local community. In fact, benefitting local people is one important aspect of ecotourism.

The study also found that most of the surveyed tourists were extremely satisfied with scenic natural beauty and desired to visit again and wished to advice friends and relatives to visit in the area. This fact shows that there is a good potential market for ecotourism in Arunachal Pradesh in general and in the study area in particular. However, there is a need for formulating proper policies and guidelines so as to avert damages to natural environment. Impact of ecotourism depends mainly on the way it is managed. If it is properly managed, it can serve the dual goal of conservation and economic development.

Four

Tourism Growth and Structure of Tourist Demand

Tourism is a human activity related to recreation and travel for pleasure mainly to a destination other than the normal place of residence of visitors. It is basically a leisure activity undertaken by an individual for various purposes such as enjoying experiences, adventure, meeting new people and culture, physical exercise, escape from routine and responsibility, viewing wildlife and so on. The demand for recreation and tourism is assumed to be a function of individual's or a group's willingness or desire to engage in such pursuits (Sharma, 2004). It depends on demographic and socio-economic characteristics of an individual tourist such as gender, age, household size, dependent members, educational level, household income, motivation. It also depends to a great extent on attributes of a destination (landscape, accessibility, and climate, attitude of local people, wildlife, political and social environment) as well as on facilities and services available at the destinations (transport, accommodation facilities, communication, food and beverages, handicrafts, services, hospitality). Costs of services available and travel cost to reach the destination also affects the demand for tourism in any destination.

The main objective of the tourists in choosing a particular destination is to maximize utility. The utility, on the other hand, is a function of both the attributes of the destination and facilities and services enjoyed at the destination such as, accommodation, food and beverages, transport, hospitality and services.

Arunachal Pradesh, the eastern most State of India, is highly rich in flora and fauna. The State has a vast area under forest covers. As per the Forest Survey of India based on satellite imagery, the forest cover in this State accounts for 80.50 per cent of its total geographical area which is one of the highest among the States of India (Forest Survey of India, 2011). In its vast and varied forests, it houses diverse species of flora and fauna some of which are rare and highly endemic. Due to its geographical location, it falls under Indo-Burma biodiversity 'hotspot' which is recognized as one of the mega biodiversity hotspots in the world. The State accounts for about 20 per cent of the country's fauna. Out of 16 primates in the world, 7 are found in Arunachal Pradesh. The state has amazingly rich avifauna with over 650 bird species. It accounts for around 50 per cent of orchids found in the entire country. It is estimated that over 5000 species of flowering plants occur in this territory. Out of which, 238 are endemic to the state. It is also rich in medicinal plants and many other rare and endangered taxa (Chatterjee *et al.*, 2006).

At the same time, the presence of numerous peaks, passes, snow clad mountain ranges and valleys make it one of the most beautiful places on the earth. The State is equally rich in cultural resources. It is a home to 26 major tribes and 110 sub tribes. The tradition and culture of these tribes are added attraction for visitors. It can be regarded as laboratory for anthropological research and can attract researchers from different parts of the country as well as from the world.

These facts clearly show the State's potential for developing ecotourism. But there are many constraints and challenges for developing ecotourism in the State. Despite those challenges the number of tourist arrivals in the State has been rising rapidly since 2004 (Table 4.1).

TOURIST ARRIVALS IN ARUNACHAL PRADESH AND NORTH EAST INDIA

Arunachal Pradesh is in the initial stage of tourism development. The data on tourist arrivals in the State are available from the year 1999 onwards. The data on tourist arrivals in the State was collected from the Directorate of Tourism, Government of Arunachal Pradesh. The trends in tourist arrivals in the State are presented in Table 4.1.

Table 4.1: Tourist Arrivals in Arunachal Pradesh during 1999 to 2012

Year	*Domestic*	*Foreign*	*Total*
1999	2092 (96.05)	86 (3.95)	2178
2000	3126 (96.04)	129 (3.96)	3255
2001	4644 (98.35)	78 (1.65)	4722
2002	6878 (98.05)	137 (1.95)	7015
2003	3632 (89.24)	438 (10.76)	4070
2004	39767 (99.19)	321 (0.81)	40088
2005	50560 (99.38)	313 (0.62)	50873
2006	80137 (99.13)	706 (0.87)	80843
2007	91100 (97.63)	2212 (2.37)	93312
2008	149292 (98.02)	3020 (1.98)	152312
2009	195147 (98.02)	3945 (1.98)	199092
2010	227857 (98.53)	3395 (1.47)	231252
2011	233227 (98.00)	4753 (2.00)	237980
2012	317243 (98.41)	5135 (1.59)	322378

Note: The figures in the brackets indicate percentage of the total.
Source: Directorate of Tourism, Government of Arunachal Pradesh and Indian Tourism Statistics 2012

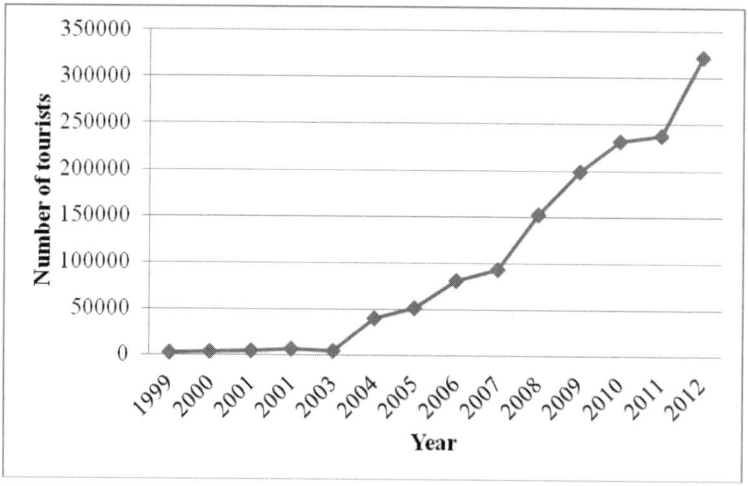

Figure 4.1: Trends in Tourist Arrivals in Arunachal Pradesh

The Table 4.1 and the Figures 4.1 clearly show that the number of tourist arrivals in the State had been very less in the initial years, i.e. up to 2003. It is also observed that till 2003 there had been fluctuations in the tourist arrivals in the State. In the year 1999, the total tourist arrivals in the State were only 2,178 (out of which 96 per cent were domestic tourists and 4 per cent were foreign tourists). It increased to 4,070 in 2003. After 2003 total tourist arrivals in the State increased rapidly to 50,873 in 2005 and further to 152,312 in 2008. In the year 2009 number of tourist arrivals in the State was 1, 99,092 which rose significantly to 231,252 in 2010 and 237,980 in 2011. In 2012 total tourist arrival in the State was 322378 which is 35.46 per cent increase over 2011.

It is observed that the State has been receiving increasing number of tourist arrivals in recent years. The growth of tourist arrivals was found to be very high. During the period 2004 to 2012, the tourist arrivals in the State grew at an exponential rate of 26.4 per cent per year. The high growth of tourist arrivals in the State may be because of the fact that in the last couple of years a determined effort has been made by the Government of Arunachal Pradesh to woo the tourists to selected tourist destinations of the State by organizing a number of tourist festivals. But there were drastic fluctuations in the growth of tourist arrivals in the State. The growth rate of tourist arrivals in the State was 26.90 per cent in 2005 over the previous year which increased sharply to 58.91 per cent in 2006. However, it declined sharply to 15.42 per cent in 2007 over the previous year. Again it rose sharply to 63.23 per cent in 2008 and thereafter declined to 30.71 per cent in 2009 and further to 16.15 per cent in 2010 over the previous year. In 2011 the growth rate of tourist arrivals in the State slowed down to 2.91 per cent. However, in 2012 tourist arrivals in the State grew at a higher rate of 35.46 per cent. The fluctuations in growth rate of tourist arrivals may be attributed to social and political disturbances.

It is important to note that domestic tourist constitutes a very high percentage of the total tourist arrivals in the State. On an average, foreign tourist accounts for only around 2 per cent of the total tourist arrivals in the State. In the year 2011 foreign tourists accounted for only 2 per cent of total tourist arrivals in the State and the rest 98 per cent were domestic tourists. In 2012 foreign tourist arrivals in the State increased by 8.08 per cent to 5135. However, its share in total tourist arrivals fell to 1.59 per cent in 2012. The relatively proportion of foreign tourists visiting the State may be due to its remote location, inaccessibility, lack of proper infrastructure, lack of proper marketing strategy and entry restrictions (as foreign tourists need Protected Area Permit (PAP) to visit the State). The procedure for obtaining PAP is reported to be complex and time consuming. This acts as a disincentive for potential foreign tourists to visit the State (Mitra, 1998).

An attempt was also made to compare the position of Arunachal Pradesh in the region as far as tourist arrival is concerned. The trend in domestic tourist arrivals in different States of North Eastern Region of India and their shares are presented in Table 4.2:

Table 4.2: Trends in Domestic Tourist Arrivals in North Eastern States of India

States	*2006*	*2007*	*2008*	*2009*	*2010*	*2011*	*2012*
Arunachal Pradesh	80137 (2.02)	91100 (1.93)	149292 (2.90)	195147 (3.42)	227857 (3.70)	233227 (3.66)	317243 (4.76)
Assam	2768824 (69.96)	3436833 (72.72)	3617306 (70.31)	3850521 (67.50)	4050924 (65.59)	4339485 (68.08	4511407 (67.70)
Manipur	116984 (2.96)	101484 (2.15)	112151 (2.18)	124229 (2.18)	114062 (1.85)	134505 (2.11)	134541 (2.02)
Meghalaya	401529 (10.15)	457685 (9.68)	549936 (10.69)	591398 (10.37)	652756 (10.59)	667504 (10.47)	680254 (10.21)
Mizoram	50987 (1.29)	43161 (0.91)	55924 (1.09)	56651 (0.99)	57292 (0.93)	62174 (0.98)	64249 (0.96)
Nagaland	15850 (0.40)	22085 (0.47)	46513 (0.90)	20953 (0.37)	21094 (0.34)	25391 (0.40)	35915 (0.54)
Sikkim	292486 (7.39)	329075 (6.96)	368451 (7.16)	547810 (9.60)	700011 (11.35)	552453 (8.67)	558538 (8.38)
Tripura	230645 (5.83)	244795 (5.18)	245438 (4.77)	317541 (5.57)	342273 (5.55)	359515 (5.64)	361786 (5.43)
NER Total	3957442 (100)	4726218 (100)	5145011 (100)	5704250 (100)	6166269 (100)	6374254 (100)	6663933 (100)

Note: 1. Figures in the bracket indicate percentage of the NER total.
Source: Indian Tourism Statistics (2006-2012)

The analysis of the data shows that Assam accounts for major share in domestic tourist arrivals in the region followed by Meghalaya and Sikkim. The share of Arunachal Pradesh in total domestic tourist arrivals in the North Eastern Region is very low. For example, in 2006 the State accounted for only 2.02 per cent of the total domestic tourist arrivals in the North Eastern Region of India. However, its share has been improving over the years. Its share improved to 3.42 per cent in 2009 and further improved to 3.70 per cent in 2010. In 2012 the share of the State in domestic tourist arrivals in the region improved to 4.76 per cent (Table 4.2). Arunachal Pradesh is ranked fifth among the eight States of North Eastern Region of India in terms of its share in domestic tourist arrivals in 2012. The share of the State in the total domestic tourist arrivals in the region may be small because of its remoteness, infrastructural deficiency, lack of proper marketing strategy and entry formalities (as domestic tourists need to obtain Inner Line Permit (ILP) to visit the State).

At attempt was also made to calculate the growth rate of domestic tourist arrivals in different States of North Eastern Region during the period 2006 to 2012. The growth rate of tourist arrivals was calculated in the following equations:

$$\text{Log } TA = a + bt$$

Where, TA = tourist arrivals
t = time in years

During the period 2006 to 2012 the yearly average growth rate of domestic tourist arrivals in Arunachal Pradesh was found to be the highest among the States of North Eastern Region of India. During this period, the yearly average growth rate of domestic tourist arrivals in the State was 23 per cent. It was followed by Sikkim (12.9%) and Meghalaya (9%). The lowest yearly average growth rate of domestic tourist arrivals was recorded by Manipur (3.6%). During the same period, the region as a whole recorded 8.4 per cent yearly average growth of domestic tourist arrivals. Thus, it is found that tourist arrival in Arunachal Pradesh is growing at a faster rate which indicates that the State is emerging as one of the attractive destinations for tourists.

NATURE AND STRUCTURE OF TOURIST DEMAND

The nature and structure of demand of the surveyed tourists was examined in relation to their income, occupation, educational level and demographic characteristics such as age, gender. An attempt was also made to study the main purpose of visit, number of visiting members and duration of stay of the surveyed tourists. The analysis of the data revealed that most of the domestic tourists were budget tourists. It was found that a good percentage of the surveyed domestic tourists (39.57%) belonged to annual household income group of ₹ 2.5-5 lakhs. They preferred to enjoy facilities at chdi:eaper costs. It was also found that most of the surveyed domestic tourists had desire to travel by public means of transport. On the other hand, majority of the surveyed foreign tourists belonged to high income group. It was found that 67.74 per cent of the surveyed foreign tourists were having annual household income of ₹ 60 lakhs and above. During the survey, it was observed that most of the foreign tourists preferred better facilities. At the same time, it was found that a good number of surveyed foreign tourists expressed their willingness to avail home-stay facilities and suggested for developing such facilities. This indicates that they are more interested to know and study the culture of the local people.

The present study also examined the mode of transport used by the surveyed tourists to visit from their place of residence. The mode of transport used by the surveyed tourists to visit the study area from their place of residence is presented in Table 4.3.

Table 4.3: Mode of Transport Used by Tourists to Visit

Mode of Transport	*Domestic (%)*	*Foreign (%)*	*Total (%)*
Roadways only	17.63	0	15.86
Roadways and Railways	27.7	0	24.92
Roadways and Airways	49.28	83.9	52.75
Roadways, Railways and Airways	5.4	16.1	6.47

Source: Survey Data, 2009-2011.

The principle mode of transport to visit the study area is roadways. Due to inadequate public transport facilities, most of the tourists hired vehicle from Guwahati and Tezpur in Assam to visit the study area. The data on mode of transport used by the surveyed tourists showed that a good percentage of domestic tourists (49.28%) used both roadways and airways to visit the study area from their place of residence followed by both roadways and railways (27.70%). On the other hand, a very high percentage of surveyed foreign tourists (83.90%) used both roadways and airways and the rest 16.10 per cent used roadways, railways and airways to visit the study area from their place of residence (Table 4.3). Roadway is the principle mode of transportation to visit the study area. However, most of the surveyed tourists were not at all satisfied with condition of roads and transport facilities and suggested for its improvement. It was found that 72.70 per cent of the surveyed domestic tourists and 42 per cent of the surveyed foreign tourists suggested for improving condition of roads and transport facilities (Table 3.5 and Table 3.6). In fact, a good number of surveyed tourists opined in their interview that the first and the foremost requirement were to improve transport facilities and road condition for development of tourism in the State.

Occupation is also a crucial factor determining the demand for tourism. It was observed that most of the surveyed tourists (54.37%) were salaried employees (Table 4.4).

Table 4.4: Classification of Tourists by Occupation

Occupation	*Domestic (%)*	*Foreign (%)*	*Total (%)*
Salaried Employee (Government/Private)	55.4	45.16	54.37
Self-employed	16.91	6.45	15.86
Professional/Consultant	12.23	32.26	14.24
Any other	15.47	16.13	15.53
Total	100	100	100

Source: Survey Data, 2009-2011.

Among the surveyed domestic tourists 55.40 per cent were salaried employees followed by self-employed (16.91%). While among the surveyed foreign tourists 45.16 per cent belonged to salaried employee category followed by professional and consultant (32.26%). It is clear that majority of the surveyed tourist belonged to fixed source of income. Hence, there is a need to develop tourism facilities in keeping view of the tourists' demand in relation to their income and requirements. Hence, there is need to develop both modest and luxury facilities taking into account the demand from tourists belonging to different income category.

Age is also one of the important factors that influence the nature of tourist demand. The analysis of age profile of the surveyed tourists revealed that a good percentage of the surveyed domestic tourists (45.32%) belonged to age group of 25-35 years and 35-45 years. On the other hand, most of the surveyed foreign tourists (51.61%) belonged to the age group of 60 and above. The average age of the surveyed domestic tourists was found to be 41.17 years and that of the surveyed foreign tourists was found to be 53.43 years. Although the average age of the surveyed foreign tourists was somewhat high, yet most of them expressed willingness to participate in adventure activities. It was found that 56.60 per cent of domestic tourists and 61.30 per cent of foreign tourists were willing to participate in adventure activities like trekking, river rafting, paragliding etc. if proper facilities were developed. This fact emphasizes that there is a need to develop facilities for adventure tourism activities to cater to the demand of adventure lovers and to attract energetic and youthful tourists in future. This will provide avenues of employment opportunities and income to the local youth population.

Education level is also an important factor that influences the nature of demand for tourism. Therefore, an attempt was also made to know the educational level of surveyed tourists in terms of years of schooling. It was found that most of the surveyed tourists were highly educated. The details of educational qualification of the surveyed tourists are presented in Table 4.5.

Among the surveyed domestic tourists, majority of them (57.55%) had completed 15 years of education, 31.29 per cent had completed 17 years of education, 2.88 per cent had completed more than 17 years of education. On the other hand, most of the surveyed foreign tourists (61.29%) had completed 17 years of education, 19.35 per cent completed more than 17 years of education,

Table 4.5: Classification of Tourists in Terms of Years of Schooling

Years of Schooling	*Domestic (%)*	*Foreign (%)*
Up to 12 years	8.27	3.23
Up to 15 years	57.55	16.13
Up to 17 years	31.29	61.29
More than 17 years	2.88	19.35

Source: Survey Data, 2009-2011.

16.13 per cent completed 15 years of schooling and 3.23 per cent completed 12 years of schooling.

The study also made an attempt to know the main motivation of surveyed tourists in visiting the study area. For this purpose, surveyed tourists were asked to indicate their main purpose of visit to the study area from the following options:

(i) To enjoy natural beauty/Recreation
(ii) For adventure tourism
(iii) To know the people and culture
(iv) Education values and
(v) Any other purpose

The responses of the surveyed tourists relating to their main purpose of visit in the study area are presented in Table 4.6.

Table 4.6: Main Purpose of Visit of Tourists

Purpose of Visit	*Domestic (%)*	*Foreign (%)*	*Total (%)*
To Enjoy Natural Beauty/Recreation	72.66	19.35	67.31
For Adventure Tourism	5.76	12.9	6.47
To Know People and their Culture	15.11	54.84	19.09
Any other Purpose	6.48	12.91	7.12

Source: Survey Data, 2009-2011.

The study of the purpose of visit of surveyed tourists shows that tourists are mainly attracted to the study area by its pristine natural beauty and tribal culture. It is clear from the above table that most of the surveyed tourists (67.31%) came to the study area to enjoy natural beauty/recreation followed by to know people and their culture (19.09%). The relatively low proportion of surveyed tourists was visiting for any other purpose which includes education value, religious purpose, official purpose, social work etc.

The purpose of visit of surveyed domestic and foreign tourists was found to differ significantly. It was found that most of the surveyed domestic tourists (72.66%) came to enjoy natural beauty/ recreation. On the other hand, most of the surveyed foreign tourists (54.84%) came to know people and their culture (Table 4.6). It can be inferred that foreign tourists are more interested to know and study tribal culture than the domestic tourists.

The study also made an attempt to examine seasonality of tourist arrivals in Arunachal Pradesh. This was considered necessary to understand the demand for tourism in different seasons. This is expected to serve as guide for development of tourist facilities in conformity with tourists' demand. Therefore, the seasonality of tourist arrivals in the State was examined based on average tourist arrivals during 2009 to 2011. It showed that the tourist arrivals in the State were highly seasonal in character. A large proportion of the total tourists were found to visit the State during the period March to May and September to October. The seasonality of tourist arrivals in the State is presented in Table 4.7.

Table 4.7: Seasonality of Tourist Arrivals in Arunachal Pradesh (Based on Annual Average Tourist Arrivals during 2009 to 2011)

Tourist Type	*Mar-May (%)*	*June-Aug (%)*	*Sept-Nov (%)*	*Dec-Feb (%)*
Foreign	31.43	6.35	33.37	28.85
Domestic	30.17	19.79	27.89	22.15
Total	30.21	19.39	28.05	22.35

Source: Calculated from Data furnished by Directorate of Tourism Government of Arunachal Pradesh.

It is evident from the Table 4.7 that most of the tourists visit the State during March to May and September to November. For example, the period during 2009 to 2011, 30.21 per cent of total tourist visited the State during March to May and 28.05 per cent visited during September to November period. This means around 60 per cent of the total tourist visits the State in a year is usually during March to May and September to November period. These two seasons may be considered as peak tourist seasons in the State.

The analysis of the seasonal character of domestic and foreign tourist shows a moderately distinct pattern. For example, a high proportion of domestic tourists (30.17%) visited the State during March to May season not surprisingly in the line with school holidays as they prefer to travel with their families. On the other hand, a high proportion of foreign tourist (33.37per cent) visited during September to November season because foreign tourists prefer the colder weather which is prevalent during September to November. Tourist visits both domestic and foreign are the lowest during the period June to August because Arunachal Pradesh receives heavy monsoon rainfall (annual average rainfall is around 350 cm) which results in landslides leading to disruption of road network. During December to February season, inflow of tourist is relatively low because of heavy snowfall and cold weather in the high altitude tourist spots. However, moderate numbers of snow-lovers visit to see and experience snowfall despite hostile weather condition (Mitra and Lama, 2012). The seasonality of tourist inflow in the State indicates high demand for tourist facilities during the peak season and under utilization of tourist facilities during the lean season.

As regard to the duration of stay of the surveyed tourists in the study area, it was found that most of the surveyed tourists (78%) spent three to seven days, 11.97 per cent stayed for more than a week and the rest 10.03 per cent for less than three days. The details are presented in Table 4.8.

The duration of stay of the surveyed domestic and foreign tourists was observed to be significantly different. It was found that most of the surveyed domestic tourists (68.70%) spent less than a week (three to five days) in the study area. On the other hand, most of the surveyed foreign tourists (51.62%) spent a week and more (Table 4.8). Not a single surveyed foreign tourist stayed in the study area for three days or less than three days. The average number of days spent by the surveyed domestic and foreign tourists in the study area was found to be 4.43 and 11.39 days respectively. The significant differences in the duration of stay of

Table 4.8: Duration of Stay of Tourists

Duration of stay	Domestic (%)	Foreign (%)	Total (%)
Less than three days	11.15	0	10.03
Three days	31.65	0	28.48
Four days	24.82	16.13	23.95
Five days	12.23	22.58	13.27
Six days	7.19	9.68	7.44
Seven days	5.04	3.23	4.85
More than a week	7.91	48.39	11.97

Source: Survey Data, 2009-2011.

the surveyed domestic and foreign tourists may be due to differences in age, purpose of visit, distance travelled etc.

The study also made an attempt to understand the type of accommodation facilities availed by the surveyed tourists in the study area. It was found that majority of the surveyed tourists (83.82%) stayed in hotels followed by tourist lodge (10.36%). The details are presented in Table 4.9.

Table 4.9: Types of Accommodation Availed by Tourists

Accommodation Type	Domestic (%)	Foreign (%)	Total (%)
Hotel	85.61	67.7	83.82
Tourist Lodge	10.79	6.5	10.36
Circuit/Guest House	3.6	25.9	5.83

Source: Survey Data, 2009-2011.

Both the categories of surveyed tourists preferred to stay in hotels in the study area. Among the surveyed domestic tourists 85.61 per cent stayed in hotels followed by tourist lodges (10.79%). In the case of surveyed foreign tourists, 67.70 per cent stayed in hotels followed by Circuit houses and Guest houses (25.90%) (Table 4.9).

It was found that both the categories of surveyed tourists (domestic and foreign tourists) preferred to stay in hotels. This may be due to availability of better facilities and services in private hotels compared to tourist lodge and circuit houses which are managed and run by the Government. As far as the tourists' satisfaction is concerned it was found that majority of the surveyed domestic tourists (43.90%) were satisfied with accommodation facilities. Their responses were either good or moderate as far as the accommodation facilities are concerned. However, a good percentage of surveyed foreign tourists (35.50%) opined for the improvement of accommodation facilities. As far as quality of food is concerned, majority of the surveyed foreign tourists (51.60%) considered it to be moderate. However, a good percentage of surveyed domestic tourists (29.90%) were of opinion that it needed to be improved.

POTENTIAL FOR ADVENTURE TOURISM

The study area has a huge potential for developing adventure tourism. The area has a number of large and small rivers which are suitable for river rafting, boating and angling. For example, the Kameng River near Bhalukpong in West Kameng district is ideally suitable for river rafting, boating and angling. The river contains world's finest sport fish *Mahseer* (Baruah, 2012) which is most sought after by anglers. Several mountain peaks such as, Kangte peak (7,090 metres) in the West Kameng district and Gorichen peak (6,488 metres) in the Tawang district which provide an opportunity for climbers to fulfil their dreams (Mitra and Lama, 2012). The study area is also known for numerous mountain passes such as, Bomdila pass, Sela pass, Bumla pass, Lumla pass which can be used for trekking. There are numerous mountain lakes in the area. The most popular lakes are Sela lake, Bangachanga lake and Sangetsar lake (Madhuri lake) in Tawang district. These lakes are considered to be highly sacred by the local people and are important tourist attractions. Thus, tourist activities like mountaineering, trekking, boating, river rafting and angling can be catered for in the area.

TOURISTS' WILLINGNESS TO PARTICIPATE IN ADVENTURE TOURISM

Since the Study area has a good potential for developing adventure activities, an attempt was made to examine surveyed tourists' willingness to participate in adventure activities. During the survey tourists were asked whether the selected tourist spots are suitable for adventure activities or not. It was found that a very high percentage of both the categories of tourists (81.2 per cent domestic tourists and 96.8 per cent of foreign tourists) viewed that the selected tourist spots are suitable for developing adventure activities such as trekking, river rafting, paragliding, angling, rope ways, rock climbing, bungee jumping, ice skating. During the survey tourists were also asked whether they would be interested to participate in adventure activities, if proper facilities are developed. A high percentage of surveyed tourists were found to be interested in participating in adventure activities. The result showed that 56.60 per cent of the surveyed domestic tourists and 61.30 per cent of the surveyed foreign tourists were interested to participate in adventure activities. The details are presented in Table 4.10

Table 4.10: Tourists' Willingness to Participate in Adventure Activities

Type of Adventure Activities	*Domestic (%)*	*Foreign (%)*	*Total (%)*
Trekking	51.76	61.9	52.88
River Rafting	20.00	14.29	19.37
Angling	0.59	4.76	1.05
Paragliding	15.88	9.52	15.18
Other Adventure Activities	11.77	9.52	11.52

Source: Survey Data, 2009-2011.

Regarding the type of adventure activities, it was found that most of the surveyed tourists who were interested to participate in adventure activities were mainly interested in trekking (52.88%) followed by river rafting (19.37%) and paragliding (15.18%). Only a small percentage of surveyed tourists showed interest in angling and other activities which include cycling, rock climbing, bungee jumping, ropeways, ice skating etc. It is surprising to note that very few tourists were interested for angling. This may be due to inadequate information and poor facilities.

Majority of both the categories of the surveyed tourists showed their interest to participate in trekking. Among the surveyed domestic tourists 51.76 per cent were interested to participate in trekking followed by river rafting (20%). Among the surveyed foreign tourists (61.90%) were also interested to participate in trekking followed river rafting (14.29%).

TOURISTS' WILLINGNESS TO PAY FOR ADVENTURE TOURISM

An attempt was also made to elicit tourists' willingness to pay to participate in adventure activities of their choice if proper facilities were developed. During the survey, tourists were asked an open ended question regarding their willingness to pay for adventure activities. The detailed results of the analysis for WTP and type of adventure activities are presented in Table 4.11.

Table 4.11: Mean WTP of Tourists to Participate in Adventure Activities

Type of Adventure Activity	*Mean WTP (in ₹)*	
	Domestic	*Foreign*
Trekking	4738	14474
River Rafting	1122	1067
Angling	768	529
Paragliding	1478	700

Source: Survey Data, 2009-2011.

The mean WTP to participate in adventure tourism was calculated to be ₹ 4513 for domestic tourists and ₹ 14343 for foreign tourists. The mean WTP for trekking was found to be the highest among the various adventure activities. The mean WTP for trekking was calculated to be ₹ 4738 for domestic tourists and ₹ 14474 for foreign tourists (Table 4.11). Hence, it calls for developing trekking and river rafting facilities in the selected tourist spots in the State.

COMPOSITION OF SURVEYED TOURISTS EXPENDITURE

Finally, an attempt was made to examine the composition of expenditure of the surveyed tourists in the study area. The analysis of data on expenditure pattern of the tourists in the study area revealed that the tourists spent the highest percentage of total expenditure (52.88%) on accommodation followed by food and beverages (38.37%). It was found that the surveyed tourists spent only 3.58 per cent of total expenditure on local transport. This indicates that most of the tourists hired vehicles mostly from Guwahati and Tezpur in Assam to visit the study area. The non-availability of adequate public transport facilities might have prompted them for hiring vehicles from Guwahati and Tezpur in Assam. On the other hand, a study in Sikkim shows that tourists spend more than 30 per cent of the total expenditure on local transport because of easy availability of tourist taxis in Sikkim (Government of Sikkim, 2006). The surveyed tourists spent 5.17 per cent of total expenditure on miscellaneous items which mainly includes purchase of handicrafts showing that there is a good potential market for indigenous handicraft products (Mitra, 2009).

Table 4.12: Expenditure Pattern of Tourists

Heads of Expenditure	*Domestic (%)*	*Foreign (%)*	*Total (%)*
Accommodation	52.36	55.88	52.88
Food and Beverages	38.56	37.26	38.37
Local Transport	3.98	1.29	3.58
Miscellaneous	5.1	5.57	5.17
Total	100	100	100

Source: Survey data, 2009-11.

The same pattern of expenditure was observed for both the categories of surveyed tourists. The domestic tourists spent 52.26 per cent of total expenditure on accommodation followed by food and beverages (38.56%). The foreign tourists spent 55.88 per cent of total expenditure on accommodation followed by food and beverages (37.26%).

The above analysis and discussion clearly shows that there is an ample opportunity for developing ecotourism in the study area as well as in the State. This is supported by the fact that the State has been receiving increasing number of tourist arrivals in recent years. At the same time, majority of surveyed tourists came to the study area to enjoy natural beauty and recreation. The annual growth rate of tourist arrivals in the state has been very high since 2005. However, there is a need to improve transport and other facilities to increase tourists' satisfaction level and to attract more tourists in future.

The analysis also shows that there is a good market for adventure tourism in the study area. It is evident from the fact that a very high percentage of the surveyed tourists considered the study area suitable for adventure activities and expressed their interest to participate in such activities. The surveyed tourists were also willing to pay a significant amount to participate in adventure activities. This fact emphasizes that there is a need to develop facilities to organize adventure activities to attract more tourists from different parts of the country as well as rest of the world. This will generate employment and income opportunities for local people. In the initial stage, the private investors may be reluctant to invest in developing facilities for adventure activities. Hence, the Government should undertake investment in developing such facilities while the management may be handed over to private parties. However, investment to develop facilities for adventure activities has to be based primarily on cost-benefit analysis. This is important for the investors as well as for sustainability of the projects.

The analysis of composition of expenditure of the surveyed tourists in the study area showed that tourists spent very less percentage of total expenditure on local transport. This is because of the fact that most of the tourists hire vehicles from Assam to visit the study area. Since the State does not have any railway station and airport, tourists have to travel through Assam to visit the State. This is a matter of concern which needs to be addressed for the benefit local transport operators.

Five

Estimation of the Recreational and Ecotourism Value

Natural environment provides a number of values. These values are classified into use value and non-use value. Use value is the value derived from actual consumption of environmental goods. It includes benefits from use of fuel wood from forests, timbers, minerals from the earth, water from rivers or underground, non-timber forest products, recreation and so on. On the other hand, non-use value is a value associated with a gain in a person's utility without the person actually using the natural resources. It can be grouped into three categories; existence value, altruistic value and bequest value (Kadekodi, 2001). Non-use value of natural environment sometimes exceeds use value. A cost-benefit analysis of ecosystems richest in species diversity leads to the conclusion that non-use values often outweigh the values of conventional uses (clear-cutting, pasture, etc.), but are hardly considered in development decisions (Gossling, 1999). Therefore, tourism and its high direct use value can play an important role as an incentive for protection of natural environment.

Tourism is one aspect of the numerous values provided by environmental goods. It is the value derived from direct but non-consumptive use of the environmental goods such as forests, natural reserves and natural scenic beauty. It is associated with the benefits derived from recreational activities like tourism, viewing wildlife, enjoying natural beauty in natural areas such as, forests, natural reserves and National Parks etc. Natural resources are potential ecotourism areas. However, the economic benefits of ecotourism areas are not accurately known because of non-availability of the market price. Therefore, economic valuation of recreational sites is important to make a convincing case for the conservation of the ecosystem. In the absence of market, economic values of such resources are measured by non-market valuation techniques.

The travel cost method (TCM) and contingent valuation method (CVM) are commonly used to estimate the economic benefits received by participants in outdoor recreation (Carson *et al.*, 1996). Several studies (Tobias and Mendelsohn, 1991; Menkhaus and Lober, 1996; Lee *et al.* 1998; Ly, 2006; Yacob *et al.* 2009) have been conducted to estimate the value of ecotourism resources using these non-market valuation methods. While both the TCM and the CVM can be used to value the same outdoor recreation good (i.e. outdoor activities such as wildlife viewing, hiking and rafting), they use different statistical and surveying approaches which have implications for the benefits that are estimated. In the present study, both the TCM and the CVM were used to estimate the recreational value of tourist spots in Tawang and West Kameng districts of Arunachal Pradesh.

The travel cost method is a revealed preference method. It is probably the oldest and one of the most popular revealed preference based methods used in non-marketed valuation. This method has frequently been used for valuation of recreational sites since it was conceived by Hotelling in 1947 (Guha and Ghosh, 2009). The TCM is widely used for estimating the benefits of access to natural areas such as natural reserves, National Parks for tourism and recreation, in the absence of market measures of these. Many empirical studies have been conducted both in developed and developing countries using the TCM to estimate the recreational value of environmental amenities (Tobias and Mendelsohn 1991; Tisdell *et al.* 2000; Driml, 2002; Chen *et al.* 2004). The TCM has generally been preferred to estimate economic use values over other non-market methods because of its behavioural base, although it is not free from limitations. This tool estimates recreation and ecotourism benefits of a protected area based upon observed travel expenses by visitors to a natural area (Menkhaus and Lober, 1996). Visitor's travel costs are taken as a surrogate for the price that they pay to visit an environmentally-based attraction and a conventional demand curve is hence established for the non-marketed recreation benefit provided. In this method, an empirical estimation of this demand is crucial for estimating the value of recreational services offered by the site. Information on varying travel costs, along with other socio-economic explanatory variables, is used to estimate the recreational demand function. The demand curve establishes a function between the price of a good (or visit) and the quantity of the good consumed. It is usually downward sloping as at higher prices (travel costs), fewer people will visit, while at lower prices, the number of visitors is greater. The consumer surplus, or area under the demand curve but above the price, is a measure of the recreational value of a natural site.

There are two basic variants of the travel cost method (TCM). These are; (i) Individual Travel Cost Method (ITCM) and (ii) Zonal Travel Cost Method (ZTCM). They are used depending on the definition of dependent variable, i.e. visitation rate. In the present study, the ZTCM was used because most of the surveyed tourists were visiting the study area for the first time. The Zonal Travel Cost Method (ZTCM) has been widely used in developed countries for estimating the recreational benefit of natural sites like National Parks, forests etc. since 1960s. In the ZTCM, the dependent variable (visitation rate) is the number of visits made from a particular zone, over a specific period of time, divided by the population of that zone (Rolfe and Prayaga, 2007). Visitors to a site are divided into different zones of origin on the basis of political boundary or increasing distance from the site for a theoretically consistent negative relation between demand price and visitation. Assuming travel cost to be an increasing function of distance, the primary cause of variation in visitation rate from different zones is traced to their distances from the site.

In this study, the visitors were divided into eight zones including foreign zone and the visitation rate for each zone was calculated as the number of visitors from the zone divided by population of the zone (in lakh) by following the definition of visitation rate from Guha and Ghosh (2009).

DISTRIBUTION OF TOURISTS ACCORDING TO THEIR ZONE OF ORIGIN

For the application of ZTCM, both primary and secondary data were used. The primary data was collected by survey method through direct interview using structured questionnaires from 309 tourists, out of which 31 were foreign tourists. It was observed that most of the tourists were visiting either with their own family members or with a group of friends or colleagues and there was wide variation in the number of visitors in a group. It was estimated that the average size of accompanying members in the sampled tourists was 5.85. Although 309 tourists were interviewed but the total number of tourists in the sample was 1809 including both the domestic and foreign tourists. The details of the distribution of the surveyed tourists according to their zone of origin are given in Table 5.1.

Table 5.1: Distribution of Tourists by Zone of Origin

Name of Zone	*Number of Respondents in Sample*	*Percentage of Respondent*
1. Assam	28	9.06
2. North East India (excluding Assam)	9	2.91
3. East India	163	52.75
4. Central India	6	1.94
5. North India	23	7.44
6. West India	35	11.33
7. South India	14	4.53
8. Foreign Zone	31	10.03
Total	**309**	**100**

Source: Survey Data, 2009-2011

The average travel cost from each zone was calculated on the basis of information collected from the sample of visitors from that zone. The travel cost was calculated per visitor inclusive of all actual expenses from visitor's place of origin as well as his/her opportunity cost of travel time. In the TCM study estimation of value of visitor's travel time is an important variable. Hufschmidt *et al.* (1983) concluded that time is an important variable, and ignoring it can bias the final results, with the implication that excluding time costs would underestimate the total benefits of travel. In practice, a rate of a quarter to a third of respondent's wage rate is sometimes used to value the travel time (Driml, 2002). Therefore, in this study, one-third of respondent's per capita household income per day was taken as the opportunity cost of travel time.

The information collected from the visitors was used to construct demand function for the site and to estimate the consumer surplus or economic benefits for the recreational services of the site.

STEPS INVOLVED IN ZTCM

The following steps are involved in a zonal travel cost study:

(i) Conducting survey on a sample of p visitors to the site.
(ii) Defining a set of zones surrounding the site on the basis of political boundary or increasing distances.
(iii) Subdivision of visitors into different zones of origin.
(iv) Determination of number of visitors from zones j (Pj) and the relative shares over the sample size (Pj/p).
(v) Calculation of total number of visits from each zone per year.
(vi) Collection of data on population of each zone.
(vii) Calculation of visitation rates per 100,000 population or any other unit in each zone.
(viii) Derivation of trip generation function (TGF).
(ix) Construction of demand function for visits to the site.
(x) Estimation of the total economic benefit of the site to visitors by calculating the consumer surplus.

THE TCM AS APPLIED IN THE PRESENT STUDY

The trip generation function (TGF) for the zonal model in this study was presented as:

$$VR_j = f(LTCPP, TTCPP, OPPTIME, AHHI, AGE, EDU)$$

Where,

VR_j = Visitation rate from zone j.
LTCPP = Local travel cost i.e. that part of travel cost incurred within the study area
TTCPP = Total travel cost (includes travel cost from place of residence and local travel cost)

OPPTIME = Opportunity cost of travel time (one-third of annual household income)
AHHI = Average annual household income
AGE = Age (in years)
EDU = Level of education

One of the problems in the TCM study is the specification and selection of an appropriate functional form. Several studies used linear functional form (Burt and Brewer, 1971; Clawson and Knetsch, 1996; Guha and Ghosh, 2009), semi-log functional form (Navrud and Mungatana, 1994; Chopra, 2004) and double-log functional form (Driml, 2002; Rolfe and Prayaga, 2007) in empirical models. In a travel cost study, it is desirable to compare alternative functional forms (Walsh, 1986). Many studies (Smith, 1975; Ziemer *et al.*, 1980) tried to systematically evaluate the effect of choice of functional form on travel cost model. These studies established that a non-linear functional form was accepted as the most appropriate form than a linear one in the recreational demand studies. In the present study, various functional forms were tested such as the linear, semi-log and double-log models. However, the semi-log functional form was found to be the most appropriate functional form for the analysis and many relevant studies used semi-log functional form (Mitra, 2003; Das, 2010; De and Devi, 2011). The two regression equations were considered which are presented as:

$$\text{InVR}_j = \beta_0 + \beta_1\text{LTCPP} + \beta_2\text{TTCPP} + \beta_3\text{OPPTIME} + \beta_4\text{AHHI} + \beta5\text{AGE} + \beta_6\text{EDU} + \varepsilon_i \quad \ldots (1)$$

$$\text{InVR}_j = \beta_0 + \beta_1\text{TTCPP} + \beta_2\text{AHHI} + \beta_3\text{AGE} + \beta_4\text{EDU} + \varepsilon_i \quad \ldots (2)$$

In the equation 1, both the local travel cost and the total travel cost were included along with other variables (annual household income, age and education). The result of the regression analysis in equation 1 showed that though the visitation rate was negatively affected by the local travel cost but it was not significant. On the other hand, it was significant in the case of total travel cost at 0.05 level. Hence, the total travel cost was considered as a better index of price paid for recreational services provided by the study area. At the same time it was found that there was a very high correlation between AHHI and OPPTIME variables. This could create the problem of multicolinearity. So, OPPTIME variable was ignored. Finally, the regression analysis was carried out by taking equation 2 excluding the local travel cost and opportunity cost of travel time.

Table 5.2: Regression Result for Trip Generating Function

Dependent variable: LNVRj		*N = 08*
Regressor	*Coefficient*	*t-value*
CONSTANT	–8.866	–0.440
TTCPP	–10.318	–4.115**
AHHI	8.886	3.871**
AGE	1.439	3.279**
EDU	0.016	0.052
F = 10.92		R2 = 0.936

** significant at 5 % level.

It is evident from the analysis that most of the explanatory variables were significant with expected signs (Table 5.2). Therefore, the first hypothesis was accepted. The variable TTCPP was found to be negatively affecting the visitation rate and it was significant at 0.05 level which was consistent with theoretical formulation. The other explanatory variables such as AHHI and AGE were positively affecting the visitation rate and they were also significant at 0.05 level. The variable EDU was also positively affecting the visitation rate but it was not significant. The R-square and Adjusted R-square for the estimation was as high as 93.6 per cent and 85 per cent respectively. The 'F-statistic' for overall goodness of fit of the model was found to be 10.924 which was significant at 0.05 level. The standard error of the estimation was as low as 0.607.

The following observations were made on the basis of the above regression analysis:

The visitation rate was found to be negatively related to the total travel cost incurred by the visitors (which is theoretically consistent) and was significant at 0.05 level. Hence, the total travel cost incurred was considered as a better index of price paid by tourists for recreation services offered by the study area.

The annual household income was found to be positively affecting the visitation rate and it was significant at 0.05 level. This was as expected since income of a visitor was also considered as an important determinant of recreational demand. Recreation is considered as a luxury item and is expected to be positively related to the level of income. As the income of a person increases, his/her demand for recreation also increases. Further the Government employees in India used to receive many travel incentives in the form of Leave Travel Concession (LTC), relaxation of rules in airfares for visiting the North Eastern States and the like which indirectly increases the real income and encourages them to travel more for recreation purpose.

The visitation rate was found to be positively related to the variable 'Age' and it was also significant at 0.05 level. This may be because of the fact that a high proportion of the surveyed tourists belonged to age group (45 and above). It is generally observed that tourists in the middle age group of 45 to 55 years normally indulge in a lot of travel and leisure activities since they have a considerably high level of disposable income and their physical condition also permits them to travel with families and friends. Therefore, if the number of visits by the tourists visiting the concerned site in a given time period is plotted against their age, then an inverse 'U' shaped curve is likely to emerge.

The level of education is an important factor which is expected to increase and influence the earning capacities of individuals. A high level of education also increases awareness among them to come and raises their inquisitiveness and desire to learn more about the natural environment of a site. In the present study, the variable 'Education' was found to be positively affecting the visitation rate which is consistent with the standard recreation literature that an increasing education level increases visitation rate (Navrud and Mungatana, 1994; Chopra *et al.*, 1997; Tisdell, 1997) but it was found to be insignificant. This may be partly due to the fact that average education of the surveyed tourists was found to be relatively high. For such a sample, an increase in education may not result in an impact on the visitation rate.

ESTIMATION OF CONSUMER SURPLUS

The recreational value of a site is reflected in the aggregate consumer surplus (CS). The consumer surplus is given by the area under the demand curve between the visitors' actual travel cost and the chock-price (i.e. the value of travel cost at which the visitation rate falls to zero). This can be shown as presented in the figure below:

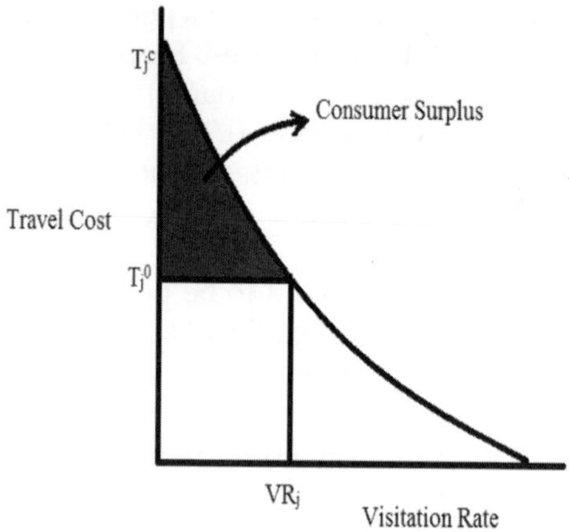

In the figure, the vertical intercept (T_j^c) represents the chock-price (travel cost at which the visitation rate falls to zero). T_j^0 is the average travel cost from zone j and VR_j is the visitation rate from zone j. For each zone a 'chock-price' can be calculated using the estimated TGF which represents that maximum of all the demand prices from that zone (i.e. the value of travel cost at which visitation rate falls to zero). The consumer surplus per visit for each zone can be calculated by integrating the demand curve between the average travel cost from that zone and the chock-price. If T_j^0 is the average actual travel cost incurred by visitors from zone j and T_j^c is the chock-price, then consumer surplus for each zone can be expressed as;

$$CS_j = \int_{T_j^0}^{T_j^c} VR_j \, d(TC_j)$$

Where, CS_j is the consumer surplus for zone j, VR_j is the visitation rate from zone j, T_j^0 is the average travel cost from zone j and T_j^c is the travel cost from zone j at which the visitation rate is equal to zero.

The aggregate consumer surplus can be estimated with the help of the estimated TGF. The TGF takes the form as follows for zone j:

$$\text{In } VR_j = \beta_0 + \beta_1 TC_j + \beta_2 AHHI + \beta_3 AGE + \beta_4 EDU$$
$$= \beta_1 TC_j + Z_j \quad (Z_j = \beta_0 + \beta_2 AHHI + \beta_3 AGE + \beta_4 EDU)$$

$$\therefore \quad VR_j = TC_j^{\beta_1} \times e^{z_j}$$

Thus, in order to estimate the aggregate consumer surplus, the consumer surplus for each zone, say zone j, can be calculated as follows:

$$CSj = \int_{T_j^{o}}^{T_j^{c}} VR_j d(TC_j)$$

$$= e^{\uparrow}(z_{\downarrow}j) \int_{\downarrow}(T_{\downarrow}j^{\uparrow}0)^{\uparrow}(T_{\downarrow}j^{\uparrow}C)\, [(TC)]_{\downarrow} j^{\uparrow}(\beta_{\downarrow}1) \times e^{\uparrow}(z_{\downarrow}j) d([(TC)]_{\downarrow j})$$

Thus, if we add all zonal consumer surpluses, we get the aggregate consumer surplus which reflects the recreational value of selected tourist spots in the study area. The consumer surplus was calculated to be ₹ 1943.21 per person per visit for domestic tourist. In the case of foreign tourist, the consumer surplus was calculated to be ₹ 5717.12 per person per visit after due consideration of multiple destination trips since most of them were found to be on a multiple destination trips. Now, on the basis of calculation of the consumer surplus, an attempt was made to estimate the recreational value of tourism of selected tourist spots of the study area. With domestic tourist arrivals estimated at an average of 130,846 and foreign tourist arrivals at an average of 2,419 during the last three years (2009-2011), this yielded a minimum value of ₹ 268.13 million which was quite substantial. Therefore, the third hypothesis was accepted. However, this value may be regarded as indicative. The numbers used are use values and do not include the option value and bequest value of visiting the selected tourist spots in the study area. Thus, the value estimated may not be proper reflection of the actual value but the concrete value has the magic power of making our mind conscious regarding the need for protection.

CONTINGENT VALUATION METHOD AND THE SURVEY RESULTS

The contingent valuation method is one of the most commonly used non-market valuation methods for estimating consumer's willingness to pay for recreation. It is widely used in estimating the economic value of non-marketed goods (Garrod and Willis, 1999) such as benefits from recreational use of natural sites (for example, ecotourism). Such benefits are typically measured by non-market valuation methods (Mitchell and Carson 1989; Loomis, 1993). The most appealing aspect of the contingent valuation method is that it allows us to estimate both use value and non-use value of an environmental amenity. This approach is used for valuation of wilderness as well as of common environmental facilities like forests, common lands, common water bodies etc. (Kadekodi *et al.*, 2000). Many studies (Maharana *et al.*, 2000; Lindsey *et al.*, 2005; Nuva *et al.*, 2009) were undertaken using the CVM to estimate the value of ecotourism.

The CVM involves the presentation of hypothetical market scenarios to respondents in a survey format, where the scenario involves some trade-off between the amount of a recreational amenity or environmental good and a monetary attribute. It uses survey questions to elicit people's preferences for non-marketed goods by asking them how much they would be willing to pay (WTP) or willing to accept compensation (WTAC) for specified improvements or to avoid decrements in them (Mitchell and Carson, 1989).

There are two approaches to elicit visitor's WTP for environmental amenity. These are: (i) an open-ended approach and (ii) a closed-ended approach. In the present study, an open-ended approach was used to elicit visitors' WTP for recreational services. Out of total tourists surveyed 71.52 per cent were willing to pay for recreational services. The rest 28.48 per cent declined to reveal their willingness to pay. During the survey, the tourists who declined WTP were asked to express the reasons for non willingness to pay. The reasons expressed by the surveyed tourists for declining WTP were; absence of proper management (41.18%) followed by Government should pay (34.12%). The details are given in Table 5.3.

Table 5.3: Reasons Expressed by Tourists for Declining WTP

Reasons	*Tourist Surveyed (%)*
Absence of proper management	41.18
Government should pay	34.12
Limited income	24.71

Source: Survey Data, 2009-2011.

Finally, the mean WTP for recreational services in the study area was estimated to be ₹ 297 for domestic tourist and ₹ 783 for foreign tourist. An individual's maximum WTP was taken to be a function of socio-economic characteristics such as income, age, gender, education and other factors. It was expressed as follows;

$$\text{maxWTP} = f(\text{AHHI, AGE, GEN, EDU})$$

Where,

maxWTP = Maximum willingness to pay
AHHI = Annual household income
AGE = Age (in years)
GEN = Gender (i.e. 1 = male and 0 = female)
EDU = Level of education

Hence, an attempt was made to find out the factors determining the tourist's maximum WTP. For this purpose, the tourists' maximum WTP was regressed with their socio-economic variables. Various functional forms were tried, however, the linear functional form was found to better fit than the non-linear functional form. The functional form used in the study was presented as;

$$\text{maxWTP} = \beta_0 + \beta_1\text{AHHI} + \beta_2\text{AGE} + \beta_3\text{GEN} + \beta_4\text{EDU} + \varepsilon_i$$

Table 5.4: Regression Result for Determinants of the Max WTP

Dependent variable: max WTP		*N = 309*
Regressor	*Coefficient*	*t-value*
CONSTANT	0.371	0.751
AHHI	0.174	2.374**
AGE	0.141	2.017**
GEN	–0.029	–0.416
EDU	0.12	1.723*
F = 5.981		R2 = 0.101

* significant at 10% level
** significant at 5% level

The result of the regression showed that the most important determinants of tourists' maximum WTP were annual household income, age and education (Table 5.4). Hence, the second hypothesis held good. The maximum WTP was found to be positively related to—'annual household income' and it was significant at 0.05 level. This was as expected since the higher income generally induced a person to pay more for conservation. The variable 'AGE' was also found to be positively affecting the maximum WTP. It was also significant at 0.05 level of significance. This may be due to the fact that as age increases people become more concerned about environmental conservation. It was found that the middle aged and older people could spare the money to accept higher CVM bids while the younger people were less willing to pay. The variable 'education' was also positively affecting the maximum WTP and it was significant at 0.10 level. This indicated that people with higher education were more concerned regarding the environment and were willing to surrender a high proportion of their income for conservation of natural environment. The maximum WTP was found to be negatively related to the variable 'gender' but it was not significant.

From the above analysis of the chapter, it was found that recreational value of ecotourism of the selected tourist spots in the study area was substantially high. So, it indicates that there is enough potentiality for ecotourism development in the study area. Further, it was found that the visitation rate was positively affected by annual household income, education and age. So, there is a good opportunity for attracting highly educated, high income and middle aged tourists who can spend more number of days to enjoy natural beauty and experience the unique culture of the State. This calls for serious attention for the State planners for developing necessary facilities in order to boost the tourism in the State.

Six

Environmental Impacts of Tourism Development

Tourism and environment have a very complex and interdependent relationship. Tourism can contribute to economic development, while at the same time it can damage the natural environment on which it is based. Today, tourism is one of the world's largest industries and is a great source of foreign exchange earnings for many developing countries. Until the middle of 1970s, research about the impacts of tourism looked almost exclusively at its positive economic impacts. However, from the middle of 1970s onwards, negative impacts of tourism were also considered by researchers. By 1980s, researchers and policy makers agreed that tourism in the way it was developed had tremendous negative impacts (Oliveira, 2003).

Ecotourism which emerged in 1980s is considered to have a potential to provide economic gains in terms of income and employment while conserving nature. It has come to be regarded as an attractive means to promote sustainable development. However, many studies (Pearce, 1985; Tisdell, 1996) have demonstrated that even ecotourism which uses natural environment to attract tourists can result in deterioration of natural environment, if it is not managed and planned properly. Others like Koens *et al.* (2009) also reported that tourism development had environmental drawbacks (such as vegetation damage, disturbance to wildlife, and an increased possibility of soil erosion) in three regions of Costa Rica. Loss of biodiversity was reported from one region. These were on account of construction of infrastructure, accommodation and other facilities for tourism development. Some of the possible negative impacts of tourism on natural environment are; (i) changes in landscape due to construction of facilities like access roads, tracks etc. (ii) habitat destruction, (iii) air pollution, (iv) increasing sewage, and (v) solid waste accumulation. Furthermore, in some situations movement of tourists leads to physical damage to natural landscape and plant and wildlife.

The review of literature on impacts of tourism shows that tourism can have adverse impacts on natural environment. The environmental impacts are among the central concern of any tourism development project (Mitra, 2003). Hence, lack of attention to the possible negative impacts of tourism may lead to the degradation of natural resources on which it depends. Hence, it calls for Environmental Impact assessment (EIA) which offers a range of methodologies and evaluation of impacts. The EIA studies in the past mainly concentrated on large scale projects such as power stations and oil terminals. In these cases considerable potential damage to the environment may justify the high costs and long time scale of EIA. On the other hand, tourism development project is of small scale and its potential impact on environment is less dramatic. Hence, it calls for a method which is both quicker and less costly to be undertaken. Secondly, since Arunachal Pradesh is in the initial stage of tourism development, it was felt necessary to identify the potential negative impacts of tourism development on its environment. By considering all aspects, the Delphi technique was considered as the most suitable technique.

THE DELPHI TECHNIQUE

The Delphi technique is an intensive and fairly specialized group problem-solving method used to harness and reconcile the knowledge and judgment of several experts. It was developed in 1955 and in the mid 1960s researchers began applying the technique to technological forecasting. Since then, its use has spread into other disciplines as a method of identifying and solving problems. It is one of the most well established means of collecting expert opinion and of gaining consensus among experts on various factors under consideration. The Delphi technique is considered as a potentially valuable tool for the identification and assessment of environmental impacts (Green *et al.*, 1990). It is alleged that the Delphi technique is increasingly gaining recognition as a means of consensus building in a variety of tourism related field (Archer, 1994; Seddighi *et al.*, 1999).

The Delphi technique has two major advantages. Firstly, the expert opinion expressed stem from individual, not from a group of individual in constant contact with each other where peer pressure and desire to conform may alter greatly any prediction given. Secondly, because the Delphi technique generates anonymity, the method can aim at gaining more candid response. Green *et al.* (1990) asserted that the anonymity of individual responses by removing the effects of prejudice, peer pressure and the desire to conform enhances the candour of respondents while simultaneously exposing agreements and disagreements. Furthermore, it is argued that an advantage of the Delphi technique lies in the consideration of both qualitative and quantitative variables simultaneously providing a framework for consultation (Faulkner and Valerio, 1995).

However, the Delphi technique like other methods also suffers from certain limitations. One of the most notable limitations of the Delphi technique is the rate of panellist attrition experienced as the survey processes (Mayaka and King, 2002). Panellist attritions are found to have considerable implications in many studies. For example, Mayaka and King (2002) confined their questionnaire to a single round due to a paucity of comprehensive and useable responses and due to unwillingness of panellists to participate in subsequent rounds. Panellists drop-out was found to be 48 per cent in (Green *et al.*, 1990) study. Sackman (1974) has extensively criticized the Delphi technique contending that it is unscientific. Woudenberg (1991) pointed out that it is difficult to assess the accuracy and reliability of a method that has judgement and opinion as its basis. Mowforth and Munt (1998) argued that the subjectivity of the technique infers that it is possible to obtain different results from different groups of experts or even from the same groups of experts at different time.

Despite these limitations, the Delphi technique is widely recognised as a consensus-building tool and has been applied as a means of cognition and inquiry in a variety of fields including land-use planning, policy making, environmental impact assessment and tourism. It was applied in numerous tourism studies (Kaynak and Macauley, 1984) in the measurement of tourism market potential in Nova Scotia, (Green *et al.*, 1990) as a means of assessing environmental impacts of tourism development. Further, Korca (1992) used this technique in his study relating to environmental impact assessment of tourism projects and Briedenhann and Butts (2006) used it to evaluate rural tourism project.

THE DELPHI TECHNIQUE AS USED IN THE STUDY

The Delphi technique is a means of reaching group consensus on an issue under consideration through the successive rounds of survey. The technique coined in the present study followed the technique of Green *et al.* (1990) in their assessment of environmental impacts stemming from tourism project in England. However, in the present study the survey was confined to a single round due to unwillingness of the panellists to participate in subsequent rounds. The most important step in the Delphi method is the selection of panel of experts (Taylor and Judd, 1994). The selection of the Delphi panel of experts should be based on expertise and on ensuring the inclusion of panellists drawn from diverse fields of experience in the area under investigation (Massey and Foley, 1987; Rowe *et al.*, 1991). Maykut and Morehouse (1994) pointed out that utilisation of the Delphi technique calls for the careful, deliberate selection of prospective panellists in order to increase the likelihood that the variances of opinion and expertise are represented in the data collected. In the present study, the Delphi panel was formed consisting of 50 members and most of them were specialists in ecology and conservation. Of them, majority were environmental scientists, botanists, zoologists, who were working on plants and animals ecology particularly related to North-East India followed by environmental geographers and NGOs working on environment. The details are given in Table 6.1.

Next, the experts were requested to identify the possible negative impacts on environment stemming from developing tourism. Experts' opinions were collected with the help of a well framed format which consisted of an extensive checklist of negative impacts of tourism on environment derived from a comprehensive literature survey. The format was accompanied by a letter to the experts containing a brief description of the purpose and area of study. The experts were requested to assign ranking on negative impacts on the basis of five point scale (five points as the highest score for negative impacts). Two months after the distribution of questionnaire, 38 questionnaires effectively assigned with scores were returned.

Table 6.1: Composition of the Delphi Panel

Panel Members	*Number*	*Percentage*
Environmental Scientists	13	34.21
Zoologists	9	23.68
Botanists	8	21.05
Geographers	5	13.16
NGO members	3	7.89
Total	38	100

Source: Survey Data, 2012.

THE SURVEY RESULTS

The analysis of data from the Delphi survey was carried out after the survey was completed. The results were calculated based on the ratings of the entire panel expert. Rowe *et al.*, (1991) argued that a group response may be calculated by obtaining an aggregation of individual panellists' ratings in the final round in addition to the dispersion of panellist opinions. Many studies (Green *et al.*, 1990; Kaynak and Macauley, 1984; Miller, 2001), however, utilised the arithmetic mean and the standard deviation as an indicator of panel consensus. In the present study, descriptive statistical tests were employed in analysing the data. For each parameter, arithmetic mean, standard deviation and coefficient of variation were calculated. The parameters were, then, sorted in descending order on the basis of mean score on negative ranking. The results of the Delphi survey for possible negative impacts of tourism on environment of the State were given in Table 6.2.

Table 6.2: Delphi Results on Possible Negative Impacts of Tourism on Environment

Environmental Parameters	*Mean Ranking on Five Point Scale*	*Standard Deviation*	*C. V (%)*
Solid Waste Accumulation	3.35	1.27	38.02
Traffic Congestion	3.22	1.08	33.69
Depletion of Wildlife	3.14	1.23	39.18
Destruction of Forests	3.03	1.3	42.99
Sewage Problems	2.95	1.33	45.22
Degradation of Landscape	2.86	1.17	41.06
Public Health Problems	2.78	1.35	48.77
Drainage Problems	2.66	1.45	54.72
Deterioration of Water Quality	2.54	1.1	43.11
Depletion of Aquatic Life	2.46	1.17	47.53

Note: Environmental parameters have been ranked based on mean ranking.

It is clear from the Table 6.2 that solid waste accumulation (with mean score of 3.35) was identified as the most significant potential negative impact of tourism followed by traffic congestion, depletion of wildlife, destruction of forests and sewage problems. The Table 6.2 also reflects that except for one parameter, the coefficient of variation was below 50 per cent for top ten negative impacts on environmental parameters. This shows an increasing consensus among the panel members.

Thus, it was found that though the tourism development has a lot of potential to enhance economic development, it can also lead to destruction of natural environment of a destination on which it is based. The Delphi results showed that how the tourism development in Arunachal Pradesh can deteriorate its natural environment in future, since the State is in Himalayan zone, which has sensitive and fragile ecology. It showed that by identifying possible negative impacts of tourism on environment, it would be possible to formulate measures to neutralize such threats. Tourism and conservation can be effectively combined only through proper planning and management. Therefore, while planning for developing tourism in the State each and every aspect must be taken into account so that adverse impacts on environment can be reduced to a great extent. In this respect, environmental education of tourists and other stakeholders can play a significant role in conservation of natural environment. At the same time, expansion of economic benefits of tourism to local communities is important as it will serve as an incentive for local support in conserving natural environment.

Seven

Conclusion and Policy Implications

In this chapter, the principal findings of the study have been summarized and conclusions and policy implications have been incorporated. The policy suggestions which have been made on the basis of the findings are expected to help in the planning for future development of ecotourism in a sustainable manner in the study area as well as in the State. However, before doing that task, it would be better to have a recapitulation of the findings of earlier chapters. Hence, this chapter begins with a summary of the principal findings which would be followed by conclusions and policy implications.

PRINCIPAL FINDINGS

Ecotourism is a form of tourism that depends on natural environment (both living and non-living). It has become quite popular worldwide because of its potential to provide economic benefits while conserving natural environment. It is believed to be a rapidly expanding segment of the tourism market. Arunachal Pradesh, the easternmost State of India, is rich in biodiversity and forest resources. The State falls under Indo-Burma biodiversity hotspot which is one of the mega biodiversity hotspots of the world. At the same time, the State is endowed with fascinating natural beauty with presence of numerous river valleys, mountain peaks and passes, natural lakes etc. The State is also rich in cultural resources. The distinct and varied tradition and culture of different tribal groups are added attraction for the tourists.

However, despite having a number of tourist attractions, the inflow of tourist in the State is found to be relatively low. The share of the State in total tourist arrivals in the North Eastern Region is very less. It accounts for less than 5 per cent of the total domestic tourist arrivals in the region (4.76% in 2012). This shows that the State, despite having a huge tourism potential has not been receiving good number of visitors. This is mainly due to its remote location, lack of adequate infrastructure, entry formalities etc. However, in recent years tourist arrival in the State is increasing rapidly. The tourist arrivals in the State increased significantly from 40088 in 2004 to 322378 in 2012. During the period 2006-2012 the average annual growth rate of domestic tourist arrivals in the State was 23 per cent which was the highest amongst the States of North East India. It was followed by Sikkim with 12.9 per cent average annual growth rate. This implies that the State can be one of the most favoured tourist destinations if appropriate measures are taken to market it tourism potential. An analysis of seasonality of tourist arrivals in the State showed that the tourist arrival is highly seasonal in character. It was found that most of the tourists visit the State during March to May and September to November period. These two periods may be regarded as peak tourist seasons in the State.

An analysis of the place of origin of the surveyed tourists revealed that the tourists were coming to the State from different States of India as well as from different countries of the world. However, in the case of domestic tourists, majority of them were from West Bengal, Assam and Maharashtra. This may be due to the fact that access to the State is easier for the people of Assam as well as for West Bengal. In the case of foreign tourists, majority of them were from the USA followed by UK, Italy and Germany.

The frequency of visit of the surveyed tourist was found to be low. Most of them (87.70%) were visiting the study area for the first time. Regarding the sources of information, it was found that print media, internet and word of mouth were the most important sources of information for the surveyed tourists. For domestic tourists print media and word of mouth were the main sources of information. On the other hand, internet and print media were the main sources of information for foreign tourists. As far as the main purpose of visit is concerned, it was found that most of the surveyed tourists (67.31%) came to the study area to enjoy scenic natural beauty/recreation followed by to know people and their culture (19.09%). A high percentage of the surveyed domestic tourists (72.66%) came to enjoy natural beauty/recreation. On the other hand, most of the surveyed foreign tourists (54.84%) came to know local people and their culture.

Duration of stay of the surveyed tourists in the study area was found to be less. It was found that most of the surveyed tourists (78%) spent more than three days. However, the duration of stay of the surveyed domestic and foreign tourists was observed to be significantly different. The average number of days spent by the surveyed domestic and foreign tourists in the study area was found to be 4.43 and 11.39 days respectively.

Regarding the nature and structure of tourist demand, it was observed that most of the domestic tourists were budget tourists and preferred to enjoy facilities at cheaper costs. It was also found that most of the surveyed domestic tourists had desire to travel by public means of transport. On the other hand, majority of the foreign tourists surveyed belonged to high income group and were found to prefer to better facilities. At the same time, it was found that a good number of surveyed foreign tourists expressed their willingness to avail home stay facilities and suggested for developing such facilities. This indicates that they are more interested to know and study local people and their culture.

The principle mode of transport to visit the study area is roadways. Due to inadequate public transport facilities, most of the tourists hired vehicles from Guwahati and Tezpur in Assam to visit the study area. As far as tourist satisfaction is concerned, it was found that most of the surveyed tourists were not at all satisfied with the condition of roads and transport facilities and they suggested for improving it to boost tourism. In fact, a high percentage of the surveyed domestic tourists (72.70%) and foreign tourists (42%) suggested for improving the condition of roads and transport facilities.

Regarding the type of accommodation facilities availed by the surveyed tourists in the study area, it was found that majority of the surveyed tourists (83.82%) stayed in hotels followed by tourist lodge (10.36%). The study of tourists' satisfaction showed that a good percentage of the surveyed domestic tourists (43.90%) were satisfied with accommodation facilities. However, a good percentage of surveyed foreign tourists (35.50%) opined that there is a need to improve accommodation facilities. As far as quality of food is concerned, majority of the surveyed foreign tourists (51.60%) considered it to be moderate. On the other hand, a good percentage of the surveyed domestic tourists (29.90%) were of opinion that it needed to be improved.

However, despite the poor road condition and absence of better means of transport and other facilities, a very high percentage of the surveyed tourists (95.15%) expressed their willingness to visit the State again, provided that the condition of roads is improved. At the same time a very high percentage of the surveyed tourists (96.12%) stated that they would share the experience of their visit with friends and relatives and would advice them for visiting the study area.

The study of tourists' perception and their willingness to pay to participate in adventure activity showed that a high percentage of both the categories of tourists (81.2 per cent domestic tourists and 96.8 per cent of foreign tourists) opined that the selected tourist spots were quite suitable for developing adventure activities like trekking, rope ways, rock climbing, river rafting, paragliding, angling, etc. From the survey, it was found that 56.60 per cent of the surveyed domestic tourists and 61.30 per cent of the surveyed foreign tourists were interested to participate in adventure activities. They were mostly interested to participate in trekking (52.88%) followed by river rafting (19.37%) and paragliding (15.18%). The mean WTP was found to be the highest for trekking among the various adventure activities.

An analysis of the composition of tourists' expenditure in the study area revealed that highest percentage of total expenditure (52.88%) was incurred by the tourists on accommodation followed by food and beverages (38.37%). The proportion of expenditure spent on local transport was found to be less than 5 per cent. This implies that the local transport operators are not receiving sufficient benefit from tourism development. This is due to the fact that most of the tourists used to hire vehicles from Guwahati and Tezpur in Assam as these places are the gateway to the study area. Inadequate public means of transport might have prompted the tourists to hire vehicle from outside the State. The surveyed tourists spent 5.17 per cent of total expenditure on miscellaneous items which mainly includes purchase of handicraft products. The expenditure pattern was found to be similar for both the domestic and foreign tourists. The careful examination of the tourists' expenditure pattern showed that the benefits of tourism were reaped mostly by high class people such as hoteliers, restaurant owners and tour operators.

The focal group discussion among the local people was also conducted to seek their opinion towards tourism development in the study area. From the discussion with local people, it was found that they were having positive attitudes towards tourism development. They opined that tourism development would generate income through increase in sale of different locally produced products and create employment opportunity for local youths. However, they called for proper management and planning of tourism so that it does not lead to damage natural environment and local culture.

Finally, an attempt was made to calculate the consumer surplus i.e. the recreational value of tourism by applying the zonal travel cost method. For this purpose, the visitation rate was calculated and the socio-economic variables influencing the visitation rate was also analyzed through multiple regression analysis. The visitation rate was found toe influenced by the variables included. Hence, the first hypothesis was accepted. Recreational and ecotourism value of selected tourist spots in the study area was estimated by using the travel cost method and contingent valuation method. The zonal version of the TCM was applied to estimate the coo:nsumer surplus. Using the total travel cost as the proxy for price paid for recreational services, the consumer surplus per person per visit was estimated to be ₹ 1943.21 and ₹ 5717.12 for domestic and foreign tourist respectively. The consumer surplus for foreign tourists was calculated after due consideration of multiple destination trips since most of them were found to be on a multiple destination trips. On the basis of calculated consumer surplus and estimated average number of domestic and foreign tourist arrivals during the last three years, the recreational value of tourism of selected tourist spots in the study area was estimated to be ₹ 268.13 million which was quite substantial. Hence, third hypothesis was accepted.

Using the open-ended approach of the CVM, an attempt was made to elicit tourists' willingness to pay for recreational services. The mean willingness to pay was calculated to be ₹ 297 per person per visit for domestic tourist and ₹ 783 for foreign tourist. The

WTP was found to be positively and significantly affected by annual household income, age and education. Hence, the second hypothesis was also accepted.

Environment and tourism have an intimate relationship. It is the environment of a particular place which attracts tourists. On the other hand, in many cases conservation of natural environment is needed to maintain sustainable tourism. Since Arunachal Pradesh is in the initial stage of tourism development, it was felt important to examine the potential negative impacts of tourism development on its environment. The identification of potential negative impacts of tourism on environment is expected to help the planners in formulating appropriate policies and guidelines to combat such threats. Using the Delphi technique, it was found that solid waste accumulation (with mean score of 3.35) was identified as the most significant potential negative impacts of tourism followed by traffic congestion, depletion of wildlife, destruction of forests and sewage problems. Except for one parameter, the coefficient of variation was found to be below 50 per cent for top ten negative impacts on environmental parameters which showed an increasing consensus among the panel members. The Delphi results showed that by identifying possible negative impacts of tourism on environment, it would be possible to formulate measures to neutralize such threats and promote tourism development in a sustainable way.

From the above findings and discussions, it is quite apparent that Arunachal Pradesh as well as the study area has a tremendous potential for developing ecotourism. However, the statistical data on tourist arrivals revealed that the tourist arrivals in the State is limited as compared to other States like Sikkim and Himachal Pradesh, which have more or less similar topography and natural attractions. Among the north eastern States of India, Arunachal Pradesh is placed in the fifth position in terms of its share in total domestic tourist arrivals in the region (Indian Tourism Statistics, 2010). This fact indicates that there are certain factors which are acting as obstacles for tourism development in the State.

After careful examination, the following challenges and constraints were found to be working against the development of tourism in the State:

The first and foremost constraint of tourism development in the State is observed to be remoteness and inaccessibility of tourist spots. This can be attributed to infrastructure deficiency, particularly transport infrastructure. Among the north eastern States of India, Arunachal Pradesh appears to be the most backward State in terms of infrastructure facilities (Mitra, 2009). For example, the State is among the two States of India which do not have functional airport. However, recently in the month of April 2014 the State has been put in the railway map of India with the completion of Harmoti-Naharlagun railway line connecting the State Capital (The Arunachal Times, 8th April, 2014). This is a major development in the State. Roadways constitute the principle mode of transportation to visit different parts of the State. However, the density of roads is observed to be very low in the State. In fact, the State is having the lowest density of roads among the eight States of north-east India. The density of roads in the State is only 21.93 kms per 100 sq. km which is much lower than the north eastern regional average of 66.08 kms and national average of 75 kms (Planning Commission, 2006). This indicates that the tourist spots in the State are relatively inaccessible. At the same time, the condition of roads leading to important tourist spots is observed to be poor and creates a lot of trouble and dissatisfaction to visitors.

Entry formalities required to visitors to visit tourist spots in the State are also acting as constraints for tourism development. Domestic tourists intending to visit Arunachal Pradesh are required to obtain Inner Line Permit (ILP) which is issued in limited places like Tezpur, Guwahati, Shillong, Kolkota, Dibrugarh etc. Though the State Government claims to have simplified the process of issuing ILP, yet the visitors are found to have faced a lot of problem in obtaining ILP. During the survey a good number of tourists (18.35%) reported that they faced a lot of problem in obtaining ILP such as bureaucratic delay and harassment. The average number of days required by the surveyed tourists for obtaining ILP was found to be 5.28 days which appears to be high.

The entire area of Arunachal Pradesh was covered by the Protected Area Regime under the Foreigners (Protected Areas) Order, 1958. Hence, foreign tourists desiring to visit Arunachal Pradesh are required to obtain Protected Area Permit (PAP) which is issued by the Ministry of Home Affairs, Government of India. However, recently the Central Government has relaxed the PAP regime in the State to open a few tourists circuits for the foreign tourists (The Arunachal Times, August 30, 2008). Recently, the Central Government has also delegated powers to the State Government for issue of PAP to foreign tourists visiting in a group of two or more members for a maximum period of 30 days (Government of India, 2009). Though the Government has, to some extent, simplified PAP regime, yet it is found to have restrained the potential foreign tourists from visiting the State. During the survey, a good number of foreign tourists (19.20%) viewed that PAP issuing process was highly cumbersome and time consuming. A few number of the surveyed foreign tourists also stated that officials were reluctant to issue PAP to them. This implies that there is much scope for further simplification in issuing PAP to woo more foreign tourists. At the same time, security forces should be trained to be tourists friendly while dealing with them.

Inadequate marketing of State's tourist attractions as well as inadequate measures to disseminate information about the tourist spots of the State is also responsible for low level of tourism development. For example, an analysis of the tourism website of Arunachal Pradesh leads us to conclude that it needs to be more interactive. The tourism website is found to be outdated. Hence, there is a need to maintain updating of information on various facilities available at regular interval. There is also a need for introducing online booking of hotels as it is done in case of other States like Sikkim and Meghalaya. This will reduce uncertainty and increase tourist inflow in the State. The success of Singapore and China in tourism industry would suggest that the marketing of tourism product is as important as its nature and quality for promoting the tourism industry (Mitra, 2009). The opening up of Tourist Information Counter at Guwahati airport in 2012 is a significant step taken by the State Government in this direction.

Tourism industry in the State as well as in the study area is also affected due to growing insurgent activities in the region and a number of 'bandhs' in the State as well as in neighbouring States like Assam which is the gateway to visit the State. Tourism is highly sensitive to the socio-political violence and disturbance. These disturbances have acted as a psychological barrier to the potential tourists (Mitra and Lama, 2010).

POLICY IMPLICATIONS AND CONCLUSION

On the basis of findings summarised above, the present study makes following suggestions for sustainable development of tourism in Arunachal Pradesh:

- Tourism development in the State needs organisational support and Coordination of different agencies. Institutional arrangements for proper coordination among different agencies should be evolved and it should be given priority in the overall planning.
- Tourism development in a destination to a great extent depends on its linkage with other tourist centres. Hence, the important tourist spots of the State should be linked to tourist centres of north eastern region.
- Public-private partnership model should be adopted as an essential ingredient of policy for tourism development in the State (Mitra, 2009). This is important because private investors are hesitant to invest large amount of fund in building facilities for tourists. Hence, the Government should build up the facilities for tourists like tourist lodges, huts, restaurants, parks etc. but the management of such facilities should be handed over to private parties who can deliver the best services to the tourists.
- Improvement in accessibility to the selected tourist spots is expected to increase number of visitors in the State. Access to the selected tourist spots can also be enhanced by improving the condition of existing roads and arranging a good quality of public means of transport from places like Guwahati, Tezpur, Dibrugarh etc. during the peak tourist seasons. However, the development of infrastructure should be based primarily on market research and cost-benefit analysis.
- The State Government should open up new places for tourists which should be linked with the existing tourist circuits. This will provide additional unexplored destinations to woo tourists. The recent opening up of Mechuka in West Siang district (famous for scenic beauty with snow capped mountain peaks, flora and fauna, lush

green valley) as a tourist destination is a positive step taken by the State Government.

- Tourism development in the State can also be promoted by organizing cultural activities, fairs and festivals with adequate policy to attract tourists from different parts of the country as well as from other countries. Hence, it calls for organizing cultural activities at regular intervals.
- Tourism development also depends on availability of professional travel agent and well trained tourist guides. But in Arunachal Pradesh, well trained tourist guides are rarely found. Hence, the Government should encourage unemployed local youths to adopt is as career option by providing monetary incentives.
- The State as well as the study area is highly suitable for adventure activities such as trekking, hiking, rock climbing, camping, mountaineering, paragliding, ballooning, river rafting and angling. Therefore, the Government should encourage adventure activities by developing facilities for such activities in different tourist spots based on suitability.
- The State has a good potential for developing wildlife-based tourism. The Government should give proper attention for conservation of its wildlife. There is a good scope for promoting bird watching, and wildlife safari within identified wildlife sanctuaries and National Parks like Dying Ering Wildlife Sanctuary and Namdapha National Park. Hence, hunting and poaching should be strictly banned and wildlife sanctuaries should be developed for facilitating visitors to watch animals and go for safari. This will lead to an increase in tourist arrivals and provide revenues which can be used for further improvement and conservation of such reserves.
- Tourists generally have a desire to purchase locally manufactured products to take away home as a souvenir. So, with the development of tourism, it could be expected that the local handicrafts may receive a demand stimulus which could help the local people (Mitra, 1998). The indigenous people of Arunachal have a tradition of artistic craftsmanship. However, there are only few shops for handloom and handicraft products in the study area.

Therefore, the Department of Textile and Handicraft in coordination with the Department of Tourism should encourage and provide incentives to local people to set up shops for selling good quality of handloom and local handicraft products like carpets, shawls, baskets, decorative items etc. This will serve the dual purpose of visitor's satisfaction as well as provide additional income to local people.

- Participation of local people in tourism related activities should be encouraged. For example, the local people should be encouraged to undertake poultry, fishery and other activities so that the benefits of tourism percolate down to poor local people. In fact, instead of importing food items, particularly vegetables and poultry products for tourist consumption from outside the State, it would be better to produce them locally as far as possible which could help the rural local community economically.
- Eco-tourists are nature lovers and their desire is to have a close association with nature and local culture. Hence, the local people should be motivated to build up locally designed accommodation facilities using locally available resources in such location to provide a unique experience to the tourists. One of the best ways is to popularise and promote home-stay model in rural areas. It will directly benefit the local people and diversify livelihood options and encourage them to conserve natural resources.
- Tourism development in a destination depends on a number of factors like its natural attraction, facilities available etc. It is observed that there is a lack of basic facilities for tourists in many tourist spots. Hence, it calls for paying attention to build up amenities like hygienic sanitary facilities in the tourist spots as well as along the roadside leading to important tourist spots. This will increase tourists' comfort and satisfaction.
- The State is lagging far behind in terms of sanitation as compared to other States like Sikkim, Meghalaya, Uttarakhand etc. Hence, there is a need to create awareness among the dwellers to maintain their surroundings neat and clean. In this regard, help of NGOs may be taken to organize awareness campaign. At the same, the

Department of Tourism in coordination with the Department of Urban Development and Planning should launch a vigorous drive to clean up towns and important tourist spots.

- Tourism development in the State can be fostered by simplifying and improving efficiency in the process of issuing entry permits. Although the State Government has simplified the process of issuing ILP by making arrangement for issuing it at the entry points, yet there is much scope for improving bureaucratic efficiency for convenience of visitors.
- Tourism and environment are closely related and interdependent. Tourism depends on environment but it can also result in deterioration of environment. Therefore, there is a need to formulate proper guidelines for tourists as well as for various stakeholders (such as tour operators, hotels and resorts, transport operators) for effective implementation of the policy and to conserve natural environment.

CONCLUSION

From the above discussion and findings, it can be concluded that Arunachal Pradesh as well as study area has a tremendous potential for developing ecotourism as well as adventure tourism. In fact, the natural and cultural resources of the State are quite congenial for developing ecotourism. The potentiality of the State for developing ecotourism is also reflected by the growing numbers of tourist arrivals. The value of ecotourism of selected tourist spots in the study area was estimated to be substantially high. At the same time, tourists were also highly enthusiastic to participate and pay good amount for adventure activities. The tourists' WTP for conservation of natural resources was also found to be moderately high. These findings further authenticate and affirm that the State as well as the study area is quite suitable for ecotourism and adventure tourism. However, it was found that there are numerous challenges and constraints for tourism development in the State as well as in the study area. These challenges are found to be responsible for relatively limited numbers of tourist arrivals in the State. However, in recent years, the State recorded a very rapid growth in tourist arrivals. This indicates that if proper and adequate facilities are developed, the State can be one of the most favoured tourist destinations. In this regard, the suggestions made in the present study based on field survey of tourists and focal group discussion with different stakeholders may be incorporated in policy making for tourism development in the State. Tourism, if properly developed, can be an engine of economic growth for the State which heavily depends on inflow of funds from the Centre. It will provide additional revenue to the State exchequer and generate additional income and employment for local people. However, tourism development in the State should be planned and managed properly so that the negative impact of tourism on its fragile environment can be reduced to a great extent.

Annexure

The Model

The conceptual frameworks of the travel cost method (TCM) and the contingent valuation method (CVM) formulated for estimating the value of ecotourism in the study area are discussed as follows:

THE MODEL FOR ZONAL TRAVEL COST METHOD

In the ZTCM, the unit of analysis is zone. Under this method visitors are divided into different zones of origin. Typically, zones are constructed either in terms of political boundaries or in terms of increasing travel cost. A visitation rate is calculated for each zone. Suppose, N_j is the number of visitors from zone j and P_j is the population of that zone, then, the visitation rate VR_j (say, per lakh population) can be defined as:

$$VR_j = (N_j/P_j) \times 100{,}000$$

The travel cost method (TCM) takes a basic proposition that the number of visits made to the site is negatively related to the costs of travel. Other variables which may affect the rate of visits include socio-economic characteristics of recreationists that enable them to travel such as income, occupation, age and education. The average travel cost from each zone is calculated on the basis of information collected from the sample of visitors from that zone. The travel cost includes actual expenses incurred by the visitor during the trip as well as his/her opportunity cost, taken as potential earnings lost for the duration of the trip. The TGF takes the general form:

$$VR_j = f(C_j, X_j) \qquad \dots (1)$$

where,

VR_j = Visitation rate from zone j.
C_j = Monetary travel cost which includes both the direct expenditure during the travel and imputed value of travel time.
X_j = Socio-economic explanatory variables in zone j.

Multiple linear regression analysis using Ordinary Least Square (OLS) is then applied to the observation for different zones (zones 1….n), to estimate the function which best describe the range of zone observations. The linear form of this function is:

$$VR_j = \alpha + \beta_1 C_j + \beta_2 X_{1j} + \beta_3 X_{2j} + \ldots \qquad \ldots (2)$$

Where X_1, X_2 ... are variables from (1) that add to the explanation of VR_j.

There are several criteria for whether the function achieved by regression analysis is a satisfactory fit to be adopted as the TGF. The most basic criterion for TCM is whether the coefficient of travel cost, $\beta_{1,}$ is negative and significantly different to zero. Similarly, whether the coefficients for other variables are significantly different to zero is important in selecting which other variables to include in the function. The degree to which the function generated explains the observations of VR_j from all zones is conventionally signified by the adjusted R^2 statistic.

In a travel cost study, it is desirable to compare alternative functional forms. Walsh (1986) observed that the double log form (equation 3) is the most often used regression analysis of outdoor recreation demand (Driml, 2002).

$$In\,(VR_j) = \alpha + \beta_1\,InC_j + \beta_2\,InX_{1j} + \beta_3\,InX_{2j} + \ldots \qquad \ldots (3)$$

Having obtained a TGF with an acceptable goodness of fit, the second stage of the analysis is to use this function to generate a demand function for the recreation site and to calculate consumer surplus for each zone by integrating the area under the demand curve between average travel cost from the zone and the choke-price (travel cost at which the visitation rate from a zone becomes zero). Aggregate consumer surplus can be obtained by adding the zonal surpluses, which represents the recreational value of the site.

THE MODEL FOR OPEN-ENDED CVM

After obtaining WTP bids from the respondents, a bid curve can be estimated. For open-ended CVM formats a bid curve can be estimated by regressing WTP amounts as the dependent variable against a range of independent variables like income, education, age and gender, etc. In functional form, it may be written as:

$$WTP_i = f\,(Y_i, E_i, A_i, G_i)$$

The linear form of this function is:

$$WTP_i = \beta_0 + \beta_1 Y_i + \beta_2 E_i + \beta_3 A_i + \beta_4 G_i + \varepsilon_i$$

Where,

WTP_i = Maximum willingness to pay (WTP)
Y_i = Annual household income
E_i = Level of education
A_i = Age
G_i = Gender
ε_i = Error term

Bid curves are useful to predict the valuation of changes in environmental quality other than those suggested in the survey, and to test the sensitivity of WTP amounts to variations in environmental quality.

References

Abhilash, M. (2006): *Wildlife Tourism and Conservation*, GNOSIS, Jawahar Park, Laxmi Nagar, Delhi.

Adamowicz, W.J. Louviere and M. Williams (1994): 'Combining Revealed and Stated Preference Methods for Valuing Environmental Amenities', *Journal of Environmental Economics and Management*, Vol. 26, pp. 271-292.

Ajzen, I. *et al.* (1996): 'Information Bias in Contingent Valuation: Effects of Personal Relevance, Quality of Information and Motivational Orientation', *Journal of Environmental Economics and Management*, Vol. 30, pp. 43-57.

Amirnejad, H. *et al.*, (2006): 'Estimating the Existence Value of North Forests of Iran by Using a Contingent Valuation Method', *Ecological Economics*, Vol. 58, Issue 4, pp. 665-675.

Archer, B. (1994): 'Demand Forecasting and Estimation', in J.R.B. Ritchie and C.R. Goeldner (eds.), *Travel, Tourism and Hospitality Research*, Wiley, New York, pp. 105-114.

Arin, T. and R.A. Kramer (2002): 'Divers' Willingness to Pay to Visit Marine Sanctuaries: An Explanatory Study', *Journal of Ocean and Coastal Management*, Vol. 45, pp. 171-183.

Arrow, K.J. *et al.* (1993). 'Report of the NOAA Panel on Contingent Valuation Method', *Federal Register*, Vol. 28, pp. 4601-4614.

Baral, N., M.J. Stern and R. Bhattarai (2008): 'Contingent Valuation of Ecotourism in Annapurna Conservation Area, Nepal: Implications for Sustainable Park Finance and Local Development', *Ecological Economics*, Vol. 66, pp. 218-227.

Barbier, E.B. (1994): 'Valuing Environmental Functions: Tropical Wetlands', *Land Economics*, Vol. 70, No. 2, pp. 155-173.

Barbier, E.B. *et al.* (1997): 'The Economics of Tropical Forest Land Use Options', *Land Economics*, Vol. 73, No. 2, pp. 174-195.

Baruah, D. (2012): 'Mahseer Fisheries in Arunachal Pradesh', *The Arunachal Times,* March 10, 2012, pp. 6.

Bateman, I.J. (1993): 'Valuation of the Environment Methods and Techniques: Revealed Preference Methods', in Turner, R.K. (ed.), *Sustainable Environmental Economics and Management,* Belhaven Press, London, pp. 192-233.

Bennett, J.W. (1996): 'Estimating the Recreational Use Values of National Parks', *Tourism Economics,* Vol. 2, pp. 303-320.

Bennett, J.W. and G.W. Flatley (1996): 'Using Contingent Valuation Method to Determine Australian Tourists' Values for Forest Conservation in Vanautu', *Economic Analysis and Policy,* Vol. 26, No. 2, pp. 111-127.

Bhandari, A.K. (2008): Tourist's Willingness to Pay for Biodiversity Conservation: A Case Study of Sikkim', in Konar, D. N and S. Chakrabarti (eds.), *Developmental Issues of North-East India,* Akansha Publishing House, New Delhi, pp. 124-141.

Bhattacharya, Rabindra N. (ed.) (2001): *Environmental Economics: An Indian Perspective,* Oxford University Press, New Delhi.

Blackwell, B. (2007): 'The Value of a Recreational Beach Visit: An Application to Mooloolaba Beach and Comparisons with other Outdoor Recreation Sites', *Economic Analysis and Policy,* Vol. 37, No. 1, pp. 77-98.

Boo, E. (1990): *Ecotourism: The Potential and Pitfalls,* World Wildlife Fund.

Brandon, K. and R. Margoluis (1996): 'The Ecotourism Equation: Measuring the Impacts', *Bulletin 99,* Yale School of Forestry and Environmental Studies.

Briedenhann, J. and S. Butts (2006): 'Application of the Delphi Technique to Rural Tourism Project Evaluation', *Current Issues in Tourism,* Vol. 9, No. 2, pp. 171-190.

Bulov, S. and Lundgren, T. (2007): 'An Economic Valuation of Periyar National Park: A Travel Cost Approach', *C-UPPSATS, Lulea University of Technology,* Department of Industrial Economics and Social Sciences, Division of Economics.

Burt, Oscar R. and D. Brewer (1971): 'Estimation of Net Social Benefit from Outdoor Recreation', *Econometrica,* Vol. 39, pp. 813-827.

Carson, R.T. *et al.* (1996): 'Contingent Valuation and Revealed Preference Methodologies: Comparing the Estimates for Quasi-Public Goods', *Land Economics,* Vol. 72, No. 1, pp. 80-99.

Champ, P.A. and R.C. Bishop (2006): 'Is Willingness to Pay for a Public Good Sensitive to the Elicitation Format'? *Land Economics,* Vol. 82, No. 2, pp. 162-173.

Chase, L.C. *et al.* (1998): 'Ecotourism Demand and Differential Pricing of National Park Access in Costa Rica', *Land Economics*, Vol. 74, No. 4, pp. 466-482.

Chatterjee, S. *et al.* (2006): 'Biodiversity Significance of North East India: For the Study on Natural Resources, Water and Environment Nexus for Development and Growth in North Eastern India', *Background Paper, Forests Conservation Programme*, WWF-India, New Delhi.

Chaudhury, P. and V.P. Tiwari (2006): 'A Comparison between TCM and CVM in Assessing the Recreational Use Value of Urban Forestry', *International Forestry Review*, Vol. 8, No. 4, pp. 439-448.

Chen, W. *et al.* (2004): 'Recreation Demand and Economic Value: An Application of Travel Cost Method for Xiamen Island', *China Economic Review*, Vol. 15, No. 4, pp. 398-406.

Chirgwin, S. and K. Hughes (1997): 'Ecotourism: the Participants' Perceptions', *The Journal of Tourism Studies*, Vol. 5, No. 2, pp. 2-7.

Chopra, K. *et al.* (1997): *Economic Valuation of Biodiversity: A Case Study of Keoladeo National Park, Bharatpur*, Part-I & II, Institute of Economic Growth, Delhi.

Chopra, K. (1998): 'The Valuation of Biodiversity within Protected Areas: Alternative Approaches and a Case Study', *Discussion Paper Series, No. 3*, Institute of Economic Growth, New Delhi.

Chopra, K. (2004): 'Economic Valuation of Biodiversity: The Case of Keoladeo National Park', in Kadekodi, G.K. (ed.), *Environmental Economics in Practice*, Oxford University Press, New Delhi, pp. 86-121.

Christie, M. *et al.* (2006): 'Valuing the Diversity of Biodiversity', *Ecological Economics*, Vol. 58, pp. 304-317.

Clawson, M. (1959): 'Methods of Measuring Demand for and Value of Outdoor Recreation', *Reprinted No. 10, Resource for the Future*, Washington D.C.

Clawson, M. and J.L. Knetch (1966): *Economics of Outdoor Recreation*, The John Hopkins University Press, Baltimore.

Commonwealth Department of Tourism (1994): *National Ecotourism Strategy*, Canberra, Australia, Commonwealth of Australia.

Cummings, R.G. *et al.* (1986): *Valuing Environmental Goods: An Assessment of the Contingent Valuation Method*, Rowman and Allenheld, Totwa, N.J.

Curtis, John A. (2002): 'Estimating the Demand for Salmon Angling in Ireland', *The Economic and Social Review*, Vol. 33, No. 3, pp. 319-332.

Das, B. (2010): *Economics of Protected Area Tourism—A Study of Manas National Park, Assam*, Ph. D Thesis, Department of Economics, Rajiv Gandhi University, Itanagar.

Davis, D. and C.A. Tisdell (1998): 'Tourist Levies and Willingness to Pay for a Whale Shark Experience', *Tourism Economics*, Vol. 5, No. 2, pp. 161-174.

De, U.K. and A. Devi (2011): 'Valuing Recreational and Conservational Benefits of a Natural Tourists Site: Case of Cherrapunjee', *Journal of Quantitative Economics*, Vol. 9, No. 2, pp. 154-172.

Dey, M. and N.B. Dey (2007): 'Ecotourism in the North-East India—Promotion for Sustainable Economic Development', in Megu, K. (ed.), *Development Issues in North-East Region*, Mittal Publications, New Delhi, pp. 1-6.

Diamantis, D. and A. Ladkin (1999): 'The Links between Sustainable Tourism and Ecotourism: A Definitional and Operational Perspective', *The Journal of Tourism Studies*, Vol. 10, No. 2, pp. 35-46.

Driml, S. (2002): 'Travel Cost Analysis of Recreational Value in the Wet Tropics World Heritage Area', *Economic Analysis and Policy*, Vol. 32, No. 2, pp. 11-26.

Duthy, S. (2002): 'Whian Whian-State Forest or National Park: Community Attitudes and Economic Values', *Economic Analysis and Policy*, Vol. 32, No. 2, pp. 91-111.

Echeverria, J., M. Hanrahan, R. Solorzano (1995): 'Valuation of Non-Priced Amenities Provided by the Biological Resources within the Monteverde Cloud Forest Preserve, Costa Rica', *Ecological Economics*, Vol. 13, pp. 43-52.

Ezebilo, E.E. *et al.* (2010): 'Economic Value of Ecotourism to Local Communities in the Nigerian Rainforest Zone', *Journal of Sustainable Development*, Vol. 3, No. 1, pp. 51-60.

Faulkner, B. and P. Valerio (1995): 'An Integrative Approach to Tourism Demand Forecasting', *Tourism Management*, Vol. 16, No. 1, pp. 29-39.

Fazili, A.I. and S. Hussain Ashraf (2006): *Tourism in India, Planning and Development*, Sarup & Sons, New Delhi.

Feather, P. and W. Douglass Shaw (1999): 'Estimating the Cost of Leisure Time for Recreation Demand Models', *Journal of Environmental Economics and Management*, Vol. 38, pp. 49-65.

Fillion, F.L. *et al.* (1994): 'The Economics of Global Ecotourism', in Munasingh, M. and J. Mcneely (eds.), *Protected Area Economics and Policy, Linking Conservation and Sustainable Development*, World Bank, Washington D.C., pp. 235-252.

Forest Survey of India (2011): *State of Forest Report 2011*, Ministry of Environment and Forest, Government of India, New Delhi.

Garrod, G. and K.G. Willis (1999): *Economic Valuation of the Environment*, Edward Elgar, Cheltenham, UK.

Gossling, S. (1999): 'Ecotourism: A Means to Safeguard Biodiversity and Ecosystem Functions'? *Ecological Economics*, Vol. 29, No. 2, pp. 303-320.

Government of Arunachal Pradesh (2005): *Arunachal Pradesh Human Development Report 2005*, Department of Planning, Itanagar.

Government of Arunachal Pradesh (2011): *Census of India 2011: Provisional Population Totals, Arunachal Pradesh*, Directorate of Census Operations, Arunachal Pradesh.

Government of Arunachal Pradesh (2011): *Statistical Abstract of Arunachal Pradesh 2011*, Directorate of Economics and Statistics, Itanagar.

Government of India (2009): *State Development Report of Arunachal Pradesh 2009*, Planning Commission, New Delhi.

Government of India (2012): *Indian Tourism Statistics 2012*, Ministry of Tourism, New Delhi.

Government of India (2011): *Provisional Census of India 2011*, Ministry of Home Affairs, New Delhi.

Government of Sikkim (2004): *Project for Estimating Sustainable Development of Ecotourism in Sikkim*, The State Council of Science and Technology.

Government of Sikkim (2006): *Tourism Statistics*, Tourism Department, Gangtok.

Green, H. *et al.* (1990): 'Assessing the Environmental Impact of Tourism Development: Use of the Delphi Technique', *Tourism Management*, Vol. 11, No. 2, pp. 111-120.

Guha, I. and S. Ghosh (2009): 'A Glimpse of the Tiger: How much are Indians Willing to Pay for it'? *Working Paper No. 39-09*, South Asian Network for Development and Environmental Economics (SANDEE).

Hadker, N., S. Sharma, A. David and T.R. Muraleedharan (1997): 'Willingness to Pay for Borivli National Park: Evidence from a Contingent Valuation', *Ecological Economics*, Vol. 21, Issue 2, pp. 105-122.

Haefele, M., R.A. Kramer, T. Holmes (1991): 'Estimating the Total Value of Forest Quality in High-Elevation Spruce-Fir Forest', *The Economic Value of Wilderness Proceedings of the Conference, General Technical Report SE-78*, Southern Forest Experiment Station U.S. Forest Service, Asheville, NC, pp. 91-96.

Hanemann, W.M. (1994): 'Valuing the Environment through Contingent Valuation', *Journal of Economic Perspectives*, Vol. 8, No. 4, pp. 19-43.

Haque, E. (2003): 'Economics of Nature-Based Tourism in South Asia', *Project Report Submitted in Round 4*, South Asian Network for Economic Institution.

Harrison, S., J. Bennett and C.A. Tisdell (2002): 'The Role of Non-Market

Valuation in Forest Management and Recreational Policy', *Economic Analysis and Policy*, Vol. 32, No. 2, pp. 1-10.

Herath, G. (1999): 'Estimation of Community Values of Lakes: A Study of Lake Mokoan in Victoria, Australia', *Economic Analysis and Policy*, Vol. 29, No. 1, pp. 31-44.

Hufschmidt, M.M. *et al.* (1983): *Environment, Natural Systems and Development: An Economic Valuation Guide*, The Johns Hopkins University Press, Baltimore.

Hvenegaard, G.T. (1994): 'Ecotourism: A Status Report and Conceptual Framework', *The Journal of Tourism Studies*, Vol. 5, No. 2, pp. 24-32.

Jakobsson, K. and Andrew K. Dragun (2001): 'The Worth of Possum: Valuing Species with the Contingent Valuation Method', *Environmental and Resource Economics*, Vol. 19, pp. 211-227.

Jin, J. *et al.* (2008): 'Valuing Black-faced Spoonbill Conservation in Macao: A Policy and Contingent Valuation Study', *Ecological Economics*, Vol. 68, pp. 328-335.

Jha, S.N. (2007): 'Ecotourism vis-à-vis Prospects of Economic Development in Arunachal Pradesh', in Megu, K. (ed.), *Development Issues in North-East Region*, Mittal Publications, New Delhi, pp. 135-149.

Johnston, R.J. (2006): 'Is Hypothetical Bias Universal? Validating Contingent Valuation Responses Using a Binding Public Referendum', *Journal of Environmental Economics and Management*, Vol. 52, pp. 469-481.

Kadekodi, G.K. (2001): 'Valuation of Natural and Environmental Resources: Methodology and Estimation', *Indian Journal of Agricultural Economics*, Vol. 56, No. 3, pp. 285-324.

Kadekodi, G.K. *et al.* (Eds.) (2000): *Water in Kumaon: Ecology, Value and Rights*, Gyanodaya Publications, Nainital.

Kaynak, E. and J.A. Macauley (1984): 'The Delphi Technique in the Measurement of Tourism Market Potential: The Case of Nova Scotia', *Tourism Management*, Vol. 5, No. 2, pp. 87-101.

King, D. and M. Mazzotta (2003): '*Ecosystem Valuation*', available at: http://www.ecosystemvaluation.org.

Koens J.F. *et al.* (2009): Ecotourism as a Development Strategy: Experiences from Costa Rica, *Environment, Development and Sustainability*, Vol. 11, No. 6, pp. 1225-1237.

Korca, P. (1992): 'Application of Delphi Technique in Environmental Impact Assessment of Tourism Projects', *Selected Papers in Tourism*, Vol. 24 (Special Issue: Tourism and Environment), pp. 46-59.

Kosz, M. (1996): 'Valuing Riverside Wetlands: The Case of the Donau-Auen National Park', *Ecological Economics*, Vol. 16, Issue 2, pp. 109-127.

Krutilla, J.V. (1967): 'Conservation Reconsidered', *American Economic Review*, Vol. 57, No. 4, pp. 777-786.

Lee, Choong-Ki (1997): 'Valuation of Nature-Based Tourism Resources Using Dichotomous Choice Contingent Valuation', *Tourism Management*, Vol. 18, Issue 8, pp. 587-591.

Lee, Choong-Ki and James W. Mjelde (2007): 'Valuation of Ecotourism Resources Using a Contingent Valuation Method: The Case of the Korean DMZ', *Ecological Economics*, Vol. 63, pp. 511-520.

Lee, Choong-Ki and S.Y. Han (2002): 'Estimating the Use and Preservation Values of National Parks Tourism Resources Using a Contingent Valuation Method', *Tourism Management*, Vol. 23, pp. 531-540.

Lindsey, P.A. (2005): 'The Potential Contribution of Ecotourism to African Wild Dog *Lycaon Pictus* Conservation in South Africa', *Biological Conservation*, Vol. 123, pp. 339-348.

Linstone, H. and M. Turoff (1975): *The Delphi Method: Techniques and Applications*, Readings, MA: Addison-Wesley.

Liston-Heyes, C. and A. Heyes (1999): 'Recreational Benefits from the Dartmoor National Park', *Journal of Environmental Management*, Vol. 55, No. 2, pp. 69-80.

Loewen, K.G. and S.N. Kulshrestha (1995): *Economic Value of Recreation Experience at the Prince Albert National Park of Saskachewan, Canada*, Prince Abbert Model Forest Association Inc.

Luzar, E.J., A. Diagne, C. Gan and B.R. Henning (1995): 'Evaluating Nature-based Tourism Using the New Environmental Paradigm', *Journal Agricultural and Applied Economics*, Vol. 27, No. 2, pp. 544-555.

Ly, Oumou K. *et al.* (2006): *Estimating the Value of Ecotourism in the Djoudj National Bird Park in Senegal*, World Conservation Union (IUCN), Gland, Switzerland.

Maharana, I., S.C. Rai and E. Sharma (2000): 'Valuing Ecotourism in a Sacred Lake of the Sikkim Himalaya, India', *Environmental Conservation*, Vol. 27, No. 3, pp. 269-277.

Maille, P. and R. Mendelsohn (1993): 'Valuing Ecotourism in Madagascar', *Journal of Environmental Management*, Vol. 38, pp. 213-218.

Manoharan, T.R. and S. Dutta (1999): 'Economic Valuation of Ecotourism in Kalakadu Mundanthurai Tiger Reserve, Tamil Nadu', *Paper Presented at the First Biannual Conference of the Indian Society of Ecological Economics* held on December 20-22, 1999, Bangalore.

Manwa, H. (2003): 'Wildlife-Based Tourism, Ecology and Sustainability: A Tug-of-War among Competing Interests in Zimbabwe', *The Journal of Tourism Studies*, Vol. 14, No. 2, pp. 45-54.

Marothia, Dinesh K. (2001): 'Valuation of a Day-use Recreation Site: Application of Alternative Estimation Techniques', *Indian Journal of Agricultural Economics*, Vol. 56, No. 3, pp. 313-324.

Massey, I. and P. Folley (1987): 'Delphi Revisited: Expert Opinion in Urban Analysis', *Urban Studies*, Vol. 24, No. 3, pp. 217-224.

Mayaka, M. and B. King (2002): 'A Quality Assessment of Education and Training for Kenya's Tour Operating Sector', *Current Issues in Tourism*, Vol. 5, No. 2, pp. 112-133.

Maykut, P. and R. Morehouse (1994): *Beginning Quantitative Research: A Philosophic and Practical Guide*, Falmer, London.

Mckean, J.R., D.M. Johnson and Richard G. Walsh (1995): 'Valuing Time in Travel Cost Demand Analysis: An Empirical Investigation', *Land Economics*, Vol. 71, No. 1, pp. 96-105.

Mendes, I. and I. Proenca (2005): 'Estimating the Recreation Value of Ecosystems by Using a Travel Cost Method Approach', *Working Paper, Department of Economics*, Technical University of Lisbon.

Menkhaus, S. and D.J. Lober (1996): 'International Ecotourism and the Valuation of Tropical Rain Forest in Costa Rica', *Journal of Environmental Management*, Vol. 47, pp. 1-10.

Miller, G.A. (2001): *The Development of Indicators for the Promotion of Sustainable Tourism*, Ph. D Thesis, University of Surrey.

Mitchell, R.C. and R.T. Carson (1989): *Using Survey to Value Public Goods: The Contingent Valuation Method*, Resources for the Future, Washington, D.C.; The John Hopkins University Press, Baltimore, U.S.A.

Mitchell, R.C. (2002): 'On Designing Constructed Markets in Valuation Surveys', *Environmental and Resource Economics*, Vol. 22, pp. 297-321.

Mitra, A. (1998): 'Tourism Development in Hilly Regions of North-East India – A Study in Arunachal Pradesh', in Roy, K.C. and C.A. Tisdell (eds.), *Tourism in India*, Nova Science Publishers, New York, pp. 175-186.

Mitra, A. (2000): 'Environmental Conservation and Demand for Nature-Based Tourism in Arunachal Pradesh', *EERC Working Paper Series, CPR-7*.

Mitra, A. *et al.* (2003): *Environment and Nature-Based Tourism—An Endeavour at Sustainability*, Kanishka Publishers, New Delhi.

Mitra, A. (2009): 'Tourism Development', Chapter 18, in *State Development Report of Arunachal Pradesh*, Planning Commission, Government of India, New Delhi.

Mitra, A. and M. Lama (2010): 'Ecotourism in Arunachal Pradesh: Opportunities and Challenges', in Islam, S. and P. Barua (eds.), *Biodiversity Conservation and Sustainable Development*, K.C. Das Commerce College, Chatribari, Guwahati, pp. 49-61.

Mitra, A. and M. Lama (2013): 'Tourism Development in a Remote State: A Case Study of Arunachal Pradesh, India', in Tisdell, C.A. (ed.), *Handbook of Tourism Economics: Analysis, New Applications and Case Studies*, World Scientific Publications, Singapore, pp. 705-723.

Moon, A. (2003): 'The Development and Application of Economic Valuation Techniques and their Use in Environmental Policy—A Survey', *Working Paper Series No. 2003-7*, Centre for Economic Studies, Katholieke University, Leuven.

Mowforth, M. and I. Munt (1998): *Tourism and Sustainability: New Tourism in the Third World*, Routledge, London.

Naidoo, R. (2008): 'The Role of Economic Valuation in the Conservation of Tropical Nature', *Conference Paper, Resource for the Future*, WWF, Washington D.C.

Navrud, S. and E.D. Mungatana (1994): 'Environmental Valuation in Developing Countries: The Recreational Value of Wildlife Viewing', *Ecological Economics*, Vol. 11, Issue 2, pp. 135-151.

Nianyong, H. and R. Zhuge (2001): 'Ecotourism in China's Nature Reserves: Opportunities and Challenges', *Journal of Sustainable Tourism*, Vol. 9, No. 3, pp. 228-242.

Nuva, R. *et al.* (2009): 'Willingness to Pay towards the Conservation of Ecotourism Resources at Gunung Gede Pangrango National Park, West Java, Indonesia', *Journal of Sustainable Development*, Vol. 2, No. 2, pp. 173-186.

Oliveira, J.A.P. de (2003): 'Governmental Response to Tourism Development: Three Brazilian Case Studies', *Tourism Management*, Vol. 24, pp. 97-110.

Pearce, D. (1985): 'Tourism and Environmental Research: A Review', *International Journal of Environmental Studies*, Vol. 25, No. 4, pp. 247-55.

Pearce, D. and D. Moran (1995): *The Economic Value of Biodiversity*, Earthscan, London.

Planning Commission (2006): *Report of the Task Force on Connectivity and Promotion of Trade and Investment in North Eastern States*, Planning Commission, Government of India, New Delhi.

Portney, P.R. (1994): 'The Contingent Valuation Debate: Why Economists Should Care'? *Journal of Economic Perspective*, Vol. 8, No. 4, pp. 3-17.

Raina, A.K. and N. Jain (2004): *Dynamics of Tourism, Concepts, Philosophy and Strategies*, Kanishka Publishers, Distributors, New Delhi.

Randall, A. (1994): 'A Difficulty with the Travel Cost Method', *Land Economics*, Vol. 70, No. 1, pp. 88-96.

Rolfe, J. and P. Prayaga (2007): 'Estimating Values for Recreational Fishing at Freshwater Dams in Queensland', *The Australian Journal of Agricultural and Resource Economics*, Vol. 51, pp. 157-174.

Rowe, G. *et al.* (1991): 'Delphi: A Re-evaluation of Research and Theory', *Technological Forecasting and Social Change,* Vol. 39, pp. 235-251.

Sackman, H. (1974): 'Delphi Assessment: Expert Opinion, Forecasting and Group Process', *A Report Prepared for the United States Air Force Project Rand, R-1283-PR,* Rand, Santa Monica, CA.

Sarngadharan, M. and G. Raju (2005): *Tourism and Sustainable Economic Development: Indian and Global Perspectives,* New Century Publications, New Delhi.

Sattout, E.J. *et al.* (2007): 'Economic Value of Cedar Relics in Lebanon: An Application of Contingent Valuation Method for Conservation', *Ecological Economics,* Vol. 61, pp. 315-322.

Seddighi, H.R. *et al.* (1999): *Empirical Identification of the Dimensions of Political Instability in the Tourism Industries of Small Microstates: The Case of Cyprus,* Department of Economics, Business School: University of Sunderland.

Sharestha, R.K. *et al.* (2002): 'Value of Recreational Fishing in the Brazilian Pantanal: A Travel Cost Analysis Using Count Data Models', *Ecological Economics,* Vol. 42, pp. 289-299.

Sharma, K.K. (2004): *Tourism and Regional Economic Development,* Sarup & Sons, New Delhi.

Singh, S.P. and B. Gopal (2002): 'Integrated Management of Water Resources of Lake Nainital and its Watershed: An Environmental Economics Approach Wetlands and Biodiversity', *EERC Working Paper Series, WB-8.*

Smith, V. Kerry (1975): 'Travel Cost Demand Models for Wilderness Recreation: A Problem of Non-nested Hypothesis', *Land Economics,* Vol. 11, pp. 105-111.

Svedsater, H. (2003): 'Economic Valuation of the Environment: How Citizens Make Sense of Contingent Valuation Questions', *Land Economics,* Vol. 79, No. 1, pp. 122-135.

Swanson, T.M. and E.B. Barbier (1992): *Economic for the Wilds: Wildlife, Wildlands, Diversity and Development,* Earthscan Publications, London.

Taylor, R.E. and L.L. Judd (1994): 'Delphi Forecasting', in Witt, S.F. and L. Moutinho (eds.), *Tourism Marketing and Management Handbook* (2nd Edn), Prentice Hall, Hemel Hempstead, pp. 535-539.

Thomas David, H.L. and G. Edward Hollis (1991): 'Use and Non-Use Values in the Conservation of Ichkeul National Park, Tunisia', *Environmental Conservation,* Vol. 18, No. 2, pp. 119-130.

Tisdell, C.A. (1995): 'Tourism Development in India and Bangladesh: General Issues, Illustrated by Ecotourism in Sunderbans', *Tourism Recreation Research,* Vol. 22, No. 1, pp. 26-33.

Tisdell, C.A. (1996): 'Ecotourism, Economics and the Environment: Observations from China', *Journal of Travel Research,* Vol. 34, No. 4, pp. 11-19.

Tisdell, C.A. (1997): 'Tourism Development in India and Bangladesh: General Issue, Illustrated by Ecotourism in Sunderbans', *Tourism Recreation Research,* Vol. 22, No. 1, pp. 26-33.

Tisdell, C.A. (1998): 'Ecotourism: Aspects of its Sustainability and Compatibility with Conservation, Social and other Objectives', *Australian Journal of Hospitality Management,* Vol. 5, No. 2, pp. 11-21.

Tisdell, C.A. (2001): *Tourism, Economics, the Environment and Development: Analysis and Policy,* Edward Elgar, Cheltenham, UK.

Tisdell, C.A. and C. Wilson (2001): 'Tourism and the Conservation of Sea Turtles: An Australian Case Study', in Tisdell, C.A. (ed.), *Tourism, Economics, the Environment and Development,* Edward Elgar, Cheltenham, UK, pp. 356-368.

Tobias, D. and R. Mendelsohn (1991): 'Valuing Ecotourism in a Tropical Rainforest Reserve', *Ambio,* Vol. 20, No. 2, pp. 91-93.

Togridou, A. *et al.* (2006): 'Determinants of Visitors' Willingness to Pay for the National Park of Zakynthos, Greece', *Ecological Economics,* Vol. 60, pp. 308-319.

Trice, A. and S. Wood (1958): 'Measurement of Recreation Benefits', *Land Economics,* Vol. 34, pp. 195-207.

UNWTO (2012): *World Tourism Barometer 2012,* Vol. 10, World Tourism Organization, Madrid, Spain.

Upneja, A. *et al.* (2001): 'Economic Benefits of Sport Fishing in Pennsylvania', *Journal of Travel Research,* Vol. 40, pp. 68-78.

Valentine, P.S. (1993): 'Ecotourism and Nature Conservation: A Definition with Some Recent Development in Micronesia', *Tourism Management,* Vol. 14, No. 2, pp. 107-115.

Vijayakumar, B. (2005): 'Ecotourism: Concepts and Issues', in Sarngadharan, M. and G. Raju (eds.), *Tourism and Sustainable Economic Development: Indian and Global Perspectives,* New Century Publications, New Delhi, pp. 69-82.

Von Buren, M.S. *et al.* (1996): 'Towards an Analytical Framework for Resource Allocation in Fisheries with Multiple Users', *Paper Presented to the 40th Annual Conference of the Australian Agricultural and Resource Economics Society,* Melbourne.

Walsh, R.G. (1986): *Recreation Economic Decisions: Comparing Benefits and Costs,* Venture Publishing Inc., Pensylvania.

Weaver, D. (1998): *Ecotourism in Less Developed World,* Oxon, CAB International.

Well, M.P. (1997): 'Economic Perspective on Nature Tourism, Conservation and Development', The World Bank Report on Environmental Economics, *Series Paper No. 55*, Washington, D.C.

Western, D. (1993): 'Defining Ecotourism', in K. Lindberg and D.E. Hawkins (Eds.), *Ecotourism: A guide for Planners and Managers*, North Bennington, VT: The Ecotourism Society, pp. 7-11.

Whelan, T. (1991): *Nature Tourism – Managing for the Environment*, Island Press, New York.

Wight, P.A. (1993): 'Sustainable Ecotourism: Balancing Economic, Environmental and Social Goals within an Ethical Framework', *The Journal of Tourism Studies*, Vol. 4, No. 2, pp. 54-66.

Wilson, C. and C.A. Tisdell (2004): 'Attitudes to Entry Fees to National Parks: Results and Policy Implications from a Queensland Case Study', *Economic Analysis and Policy*, Vol. 34, No. 1, pp. 79-102.

Woudenberg, F. (1991): 'An Evaluation of Delphi', *Technological Forecasting and Social Change*, Vol. 40, pp. 131-150.

WTTC (2010): *WTTC Forecasts Subdued Growth for 2010*, http// www.wttc.org/news-media/newarchive/2010/wttc-forecasts-subdued-growth-2010/.

Wunder, S. (1999): 'Promoting Forests Conservation through Ecotourism Income? A Case Study of the Ecuadorian Amazon Region', *Occasional Paper No. 21*, Centre for International Forestry Research (CIFOR), Jakarta.

Xue, D., A. Cook and C.A. Tesdell (2000): 'Biodiversity and a Travel Cost Evaluation of Tourism: The Case of Cahngbaishan Mountain Biodiversity Reserve, China', *Discussion Papers, No. 274* (April), Department of Economics, University of Queensland, Brisbane.

Yacob, M.R. *et al.* (2009): 'Contingent Valuation of Ecotourism in Marine Parks, Malaysia: Implication for Sustainable Marine Park Revenue and Ecotourism Management', *World Applied Science Journal*, Vol. 7, No. 12, pp. 1474-1481.

Ziemer, R. *et al.* (1980): 'Recreation Demand Equations: Functional Form and Consumer Surplus', *American Journal of Agricultural Economics*, Feb. pp. 136-141.